# CORTISOL DETOX DIET COOKBOOK 2024

Easy and Delicious Recipes to Reset your Hormones, Reduce Stress and Boost Energy.

## Grace Mitchell

# Table of Content

# Introduction

## Understanding Cortisol and Its Impact on Health

Cortisol, often referred to as the "stress hormone," plays a crucial role in the body's response to stress. Produced by the adrenal glands, cortisol serves a variety of functions that are essential for survival. However, when cortisol levels become chronically elevated due to prolonged stress or other factors, it can have profound implications for overall health and well-being.

### The Role of Cortisol

Cortisol is part of the body's natural stress response system, known as the hypothalamic-pituitary-adrenal (HPA) axis. When faced with a perceived threat or stressor, whether physical, emotional, or psychological, the hypothalamus in the brain sends signals to the pituitary gland to release adrenocorticotropic hormone (ACTH). ACTH then stimulates the adrenal glands to produce cortisol.

### Functions of Cortisol:

Regulation of Metabolism: Cortisol helps regulate metabolism by influencing how the body converts carbohydrates, fats, and proteins into energy. It can increase blood sugar levels to provide a quick energy boost during stressful situations.

Immune Function: Cortisol has anti-inflammatory properties and plays a role in regulating the immune system's response to infection, injury, or illness.

Blood Pressure Regulation: Cortisol helps regulate blood pressure by influencing the constriction and dilation of blood vessels.

Stress Response: Cortisol is central to the body's stress response, helping to mobilize resources and energy to cope with challenging situations.

### The Impact of Chronic Stress on Cortisol Levels

While cortisol is crucial for short-term stress responses, problems arise when cortisol levels remain elevated over an extended period.

Chronic stress, whether from ongoing work pressures, relationship difficulties, financial worries, or other sources, can lead to dysregulation of the HPA axis and chronically elevated cortisol levels.

## Health Implications of Elevated Cortisol:

Weight Gain: Chronic stress and high cortisol levels have been linked to abdominal weight gain and increased appetite, particularly for high-calorie, high-fat foods.

Insulin Resistance: Elevated cortisol levels can contribute to insulin resistance, a precursor to type 2 diabetes, by impairing insulin sensitivity and promoting glucose production in the liver.

Suppressed Immune Function: Prolonged exposure to high cortisol levels can suppress immune function, making individuals more susceptible to infections and illnesses.

Digestive Issues: Bloating, indigestion, and changes in appetite are just a few of the symptoms that cortisol may cause in the digestive system.

Sleep Disturbances: Elevated cortisol levels can disrupt sleep patterns, leading to insomnia or poor-quality sleep.

Mood Disorders: Chronic stress and high cortisol levels have been associated with an increased risk of anxiety, depression, and other mood disorders.

## Managing Cortisol Levels

While it may not be possible to eliminate stress entirely from our lives, there are strategies we can employ to help manage cortisol levels and mitigate its negative effects:

Stress Management Techniques: Practices such as mindfulness meditation, deep breathing exercises, yoga, and progressive muscle relaxation can help reduce stress and lower cortisol levels.

Regular Exercise: Engaging in regular physical activity can help regulate cortisol levels and promote overall well-being.

Healthy Lifestyle Choices: Eating a balanced diet, getting adequate sleep, and avoiding excessive caffeine and alcohol consumption can support healthy cortisol levels.

Social Support: Cultivating strong social connections and seeking support from friends, family, or a therapist can help buffer the effects of stress and cortisol on health.

# The Role of Diet in Cortisol Management

Diet plays a fundamental role in regulating cortisol levels and managing stress. The foods we eat can either contribute to the dysregulation of cortisol production or support its healthy balance. Understanding how different dietary choices influence cortisol levels is essential for promoting overall well-being and managing stress effectively.

## Nutritional Impact on Cortisol Regulation

Balancing Blood Sugar Levels: One of the key ways diet influences cortisol levels is through its impact on blood sugar regulation. Consuming high-sugar and refined carbohydrate foods can lead to rapid spikes and crashes in blood sugar levels, triggering the release of cortisol to help stabilize glucose levels. Over time, this cycle of blood sugar fluctuations can contribute to chronic stress and dysregulation of cortisol production.

Supporting Adrenal Health: The adrenal glands, which produce cortisol, rely on a variety of nutrients for optimal function. These include vitamin C, B vitamins, magnesium, zinc, and omega-3 fatty acids. A diet rich in whole, nutrient-dense foods such as fruits, vegetables, lean proteins, nuts, seeds, and healthy fats can provide the essential nutrients needed to support adrenal health and cortisol regulation.

Inflammation and Cortisol: Chronic inflammation in the body can contribute to dysregulation of the HPA axis and elevated cortisol levels. Certain dietary factors, such as processed foods, refined sugars, unhealthy fats, and excessive alcohol consumption, can promote inflammation. Conversely, an anti-inflammatory diet rich in antioxidants, phytonutrients, and omega-3 fatty acids can help reduce inflammation and support healthy cortisol levels.

Gut Health: Emerging research suggests that the gut microbiome may play a role in cortisol regulation and stress response. An imbalance in gut bacteria, known as dysbiosis, has been linked to increased cortisol levels and stress-related disorders. Consuming a diet rich in fiber, prebiotics, and probiotics can promote a healthy gut microbiome, which in turn may support optimal cortisol regulation and stress resilience.

**Dietary Strategies for Cortisol Management**

Emphasize Whole, Nutrient-Dense Foods: Focus on consuming a diet rich in whole foods such as fruits, vegetables, whole grains, lean proteins, nuts, seeds, and healthy fats. These foods provide essential nutrients that support adrenal health and cortisol regulation.

- Balance Macronutrients: **Aim to include a balance of carbohydrates, proteins, and fats in each meal to help stabilize blood sugar levels and prevent cortisol spikes. Choose complex carbohydrates such as whole grains, legumes, and starchy vegetables, along with lean** sources of protein and healthy fats.

- Mindful Eating: **Practice mindful eating by paying attention to hunger and satiety cues, eating slowly, and savoring each bite. Avoid eating in a rushed or stressed state, as this can contribute to cortisol dysregulation.**

- Limit Caffeine and Alcohol: **While moderate consumption of caffeine and alcohol may not pose a problem for everyone, excessive intake can contribute to cortisol dysregulation and exacerbate stress. Limit caffeine and alcohol consumption, especially in the evening, to support healthy cortisol levels and sleep quality.**

- Stay Hydrated: **Adequate hydration is essential for overall health and may also help support cortisol regulation. Aim to drink plenty of water throughout the day to stay hydrated and support optimal physiological function. effectively and cultivating resilience in the face of stress.**

# How This Cookbook Can Help You Balance Your Cortisol Levels

Embarking on a journey to balance cortisol levels is a significant step towards promoting overall health and well-being. This cookbook is designed to support you in this endeavor by providing delicious, nutrient-dense recipes that nourish your body and help regulate cortisol production. Let's explore how the recipes and principles outlined in this cookbook can empower you to manage cortisol levels effectively.

## 1. Nutrient-Dense Ingredients

Each recipe in this cookbook is carefully crafted to include nutrient-dense ingredients that support adrenal health and cortisol regulation. By incorporating a variety of fruits, vegetables, lean proteins, whole grains, nuts, seeds, and healthy fats into your diet, you provide your body with the essential nutrients it needs to function optimally. These ingredients are rich in vitamins, minerals, antioxidants, and phytonutrients that support adrenal function, reduce inflammation, and promote overall well-being.

## 2. Balanced Macronutrients

Balancing of the macronutrients—carbohydrates, proteins, and fats—is essential for stabilizing blood sugar levels and preventing cortisol spikes. The recipes in this cookbook are thoughtfully designed to include a balance of carbohydrates, proteins, and healthy fats in each meal. By consuming meals that provide sustained energy and satiety, you can help regulate cortisol levels and avoid the blood sugar fluctuations that contribute to stress and dysregulation of the HPA axis.

## 3. Anti-Inflammatory Foods

Chronic inflammation is associated with dysregulation of cortisol production and increased stress levels. Many of the ingredients featured in the recipes in this cookbook have anti-inflammatory properties, such as fruits, vegetables, omega-3 fatty acids, and spices like turmeric and ginger. By incorporating these anti-inflammatory foods into your diet, you can help reduce inflammation, support adrenal health, and promote balanced cortisol levels.

## 4. Mindful Eating Practices

Mindful eating is an important aspect of managing cortisol levels and promoting overall well-being. The recipes in this cookbook encourage mindful eating practices by emphasizing the enjoyment of food, paying attention to hunger and satiety cues, and savoring each bite. By practicing mindful eating, you can reduce stress around meal times, improve digestion, and support healthy cortisol regulation.

## 5. Variety and Flavor

Eating should be a pleasurable experience, and this cookbook aims to provide a wide variety of flavorful recipes that make healthy eating enjoyable and sustainable. From hearty breakfasts and satisfying lunches to delicious dinners and wholesome snacks, there's something for every palate and preference. By exploring new flavors and ingredients, you can expand your culinary repertoire and discover delicious ways to support your cortisol detox journey.

## 6. Supportive Community

Embarking on a cortisol detox journey can feel overwhelming at times, but you're not alone. This cookbook is accompanied by a supportive community of like-minded individuals who are also striving to balance their cortisol levels and improve their health. Whether you're seeking motivation, inspiration, or simply a place to share your experiences, this community is here to support you every step of the way.

# Tips for Successful Implementation of the Cortisol Detox Diet

Embarking on a cortisol detox diet can be a transformative journey towards better health and well-being. However, like any dietary change, it requires commitment, planning, and support to be successful. Here are some tips to help you navigate the cortisol detox diet effectively and achieve your health goals:

## 1. Educate Yourself

Before starting the cortisol detox diet, take the time to educate yourself about cortisol, its impact on health, and how dietary and lifestyle factors influence cortisol levels. Understanding the underlying principles of the diet will empower you to make informed decisions and stay motivated throughout the process.

## 2. Set Clear Goals

Define your reasons for undertaking the cortisol detox diet and set clear, achievable goals for yourself. Whether your goal is to reduce stress, improve energy levels, manage weight, or enhance overall well-being, having a clear sense of purpose will help you stay focused and motivated on your journey.

## 3. Plan Ahead

Planning is key to success on any diet, including the cortisol detox diet. Take the time to plan your meals, snacks, and grocery shopping list in advance to ensure that you have healthy options readily available. Batch cooking and meal prepping can also save time and make it easier to stick to your dietary goals during busy weeks.

## 4. Focus on Whole Foods

Base your diet around whole, nutrient-dense foods such as fruits, vegetables, lean proteins, whole grains, nuts, seeds, and healthy fats. These foods provide essential nutrients that support adrenal health, regulate cortisol levels, and promote overall well-being. Minimize processed and refined foods, which can contribute to inflammation and cortisol dysregulation.

## 5. Balance Macronutrients

Include a balance of carbohydrates, proteins, and fats in each meal to help stabilize blood sugar levels and prevent cortisol spikes. Aim for complex carbohydrates, lean sources of protein, and healthy fats to provide sustained energy and satiety throughout the day. Experiment with different combinations and portion sizes to find what works best for you.

## 6. Practice Mindful Eating

Pay attention to hunger and satiety cues, and practice mindful eating to enhance your enjoyment and satisfaction with meals. Chew your food slowly, savoring the flavors and textures, and avoid distractions such as screens or multitasking while eating. Mindful eating can help reduce stress around meal times, improve digestion, and support healthy cortisol regulation.

## 7. Stay Hydrated

Drink plenty of water throughout the day to stay hydrated and support optimal physiological function. Dehydration can exacerbate stress and fatigue, so aim to drink water regularly, especially if you're engaging in physical activity or spending time outdoors.

## 8. Manage Stress

In addition to dietary changes, incorporate stress management techniques into your daily routine to support cortisol regulation and overall well-being. Practices such as mindfulness meditation, deep breathing exercises, yoga, and spending time in nature can help reduce stress levels and promote relaxation.

## 9. Monitor Your Progress

Keep track of your dietary choices, energy levels, mood, and other relevant factors to monitor your progress and make adjustments as needed. Consider keeping a food journal or using a tracking app to record your meals, symptoms, and emotions to identify patterns and areas for improvement.

## 10. Seek Support

Finally, don't hesitate to seek support from friends, family, or a healthcare professional if you need guidance or encouragement along the way. Surround yourself with people who understand and support your dietary goals, and don't be afraid to ask for help when needed.

# Breakfast Recipes

# Green Smoothie

Time of Preparation: **5 minutes**

Cooking Time: **None**

Serving Units: **1-2 servings**

## Ingredients:

- 1 ripe banana, frozen
- 1 cup fresh spinach or kale leaves, packed
- 1/2 cup pineapple chunks, fresh or frozen
- 1/2 cup cucumber, chopped
- 1/2 cup plain Greek yogurt or almond milk
- one tablespoon of honey or maple syrup. If desired
- You may optionally juice half a lemon or lime.
- Ice cubes (optional)

## Procedures:

1. Peel the banana and chop it into chunks. If using fresh pineapple, peel and chop into chunks.
2. In a blender, combine the banana, spinach or kale leaves, pineapple chunks, chopped cucumber, Greek yogurt or almond milk, and optional honey or maple syrup.
3. Squeeze in the juice of half a lemon or lime for added freshness, if desired.
4. Process on high speed until creamy and smooth. If a thicker consistency is preferred, add a handful of ice cubes and blend again until smooth.
5. Once the desired consistency is achieved, pour the smoothie into glasses and serve immediately.

## Nutritional Value (per serving):

- Calories: **Approximately 200-250 kcal**
- Protein: 8-10 grams
- Carbohydrates: 40-45 grams
- Fiber: 5-6 grams
- Fat: 2-4 grams
- Vitamin C: 70-100% of daily recommended intake
- Vitamin A: 50-70% of daily recommended intake
- Potassium: 15-20% of daily recommended intake

## Cooking Tips:

- For a creamier texture, use frozen banana chunks and pineapple chunks.
- To suit your taste, add more or less honey or maple syrup to the smoothie to change its sweetness.
- If using fresh spinach or kale, consider adding a few ice cubes to the blender to chill the smoothie.
- Experiment with additional ingredients such as avocado, chia seeds, or protein powder to boost the nutritional content of the smoothie.

## Health Benefits:

- Nutrient-Rich: **This smoothie is loaded with vitamins, minerals, and antioxidants from the fruits and vegetables, providing a powerful nutritional boost to support overall health.**
- Hydration: **With high water content from ingredients like cucumber and pineapple, this smoothie helps keep you hydrated, especially important in the morning after a night of fasting.**
- Digestive Support: **The fiber from the fruits and vegetables in this smoothie promotes healthy digestion and may help prevent constipation.**
- Energy Boost: **The natural sugars from the fruits combined with the protein from Greek yogurt or almond milk provide a quick and sustained energy boost to kickstart your day.**
- Weight Management: **Low in calories and rich in fiber, this smoothie can help keep you feeling full and satisfied, making it a nutritious option for those looking to manage their weight.**

# Quinoa and Berry Breakfast Bowl

**Time of Preparation:** 20 minutes

**Cooking Time:** 15 minutes

**Serving Units:** 2 servings

## Ingredients:

- 1/2 cup quinoa, rinsed
- 1 cup water or almond milk
- 1 cup mixed berries (such as strawberries, blueberries, raspberries)
- 2 tablespoons honey or maple syrup
- • 1/4 cup chopped walnuts or sliced almonds
- 1 tablespoon chia seeds
- 1/2 teaspoon vanilla extract
- Pinch of cinnamon (optional)
- Greek yogurt or coconut yogurt for serving (optional)

## Procedures:

1. In a small saucepan, combine the quinoa and water or almond milk. Heat to a boil on a medium setting.
2. Reduce the heat to low, cover, and simmer for 15 minutes, or until the quinoa is tender and the liquid is absorbed.
3. Once cooked, fluff the quinoa with a fork and transfer it to a mixing bowl.
4. Add the mixed berries, honey or maple syrup, sliced almonds or chopped walnuts, chia seeds, vanilla extract, and optional cinnamon to the bowl with the cooked quinoa.
5. Gently toss the ingredients together until well combined.

6. Divide the quinoa and berry mixture between serving bowls.

7. Serve the breakfast bowls warm or chilled, topped with a dollop of Greek yogurt or coconut yogurt if desired.

## Nutritional Value (per serving):

- Calories: Approximately 300-350 kcal
- Protein: 8-10 grams
- Carbohydrates: 45-50 grams
- Fiber: 6-8 grams
- Fat: 8-10 grams
- Vitamin C: 40-60% of daily recommended intake
- Iron: 15-20% of daily recommended intake
- Calcium: 10-15% of daily recommended intake

## Cooking Tips:

- Rinse the quinoa under cold water before cooking to remove any bitterness.
- Feel free to use your choice of milk (such as almond milk, coconut milk, or dairy milk) for cooking the quinoa to add extra creaminess and flavor.

- Customize the sweetness of the breakfast bowl by adjusting the amount of honey or maple syrup according to your taste preferences.
- Prepare a batch of quinoa ahead of time and store it in the refrigerator for quick and easy breakfasts throughout the week.

## Health Benefits:

- High Protein: Quinoa is a complete protein, meaning it contains all nine essential amino acids, making this breakfast bowl a satisfying and nutritious option to start your day.
- Fiber-Rich: Both quinoa and berries are high in fiber, which helps promote digestive health, regulate blood sugar levels, and keep you feeling full and satisfied until your next meal.
- Antioxidant Powerhouse: Berries are packed with antioxidants, including vitamin C and polyphenols, which help protect against oxidative stress and inflammation in the body.

# Coconut Chia Seed Pudding

- Time of Preparation: **5 minutes** (plus chilling time)
- Cooking Time: **None**
- Serving Units: **2 servings**

## Ingredients:

- 1/4 cup chia seeds
- 1 cup coconut milk (canned or homemade)
- One tablespoon (optional) of maple syrup or honey
- 1/2 teaspoon vanilla extract
- Optional toppings: nuts, coconut flakes, or fresh fruit.

## Procedures:

1. In a mixing bowl or jar, combine the chia seeds, coconut milk, optional honey or maple syrup, and vanilla extract.
2. Whisk or stir the ingredients together until well combined.
3. Cover the bowl or jar and refrigerate for at least 2 hours, or preferably overnight, to allow the chia seeds to absorb the liquid and thicken into a pudding-like consistency.
4. Once chilled and set, stir the pudding to evenly distribute the chia seeds.
5. Divide the coconut chia seed pudding between serving bowls or glasses.
6. Top with your choice of fresh fruit, nuts, or coconut flakes for added flavor and texture, if desired. Serve chilled and enjoy!

## Nutritional Value (per serving):

- Calories: **Approximately 150-200 kcal**

- Protein: 3-5 grams
- Carbohydrates: 10-15 grams
- Fiber: 8-10 grams
- Fat: 10-15 grams
- Calcium: 10-15% of daily recommended intake
- Iron: 10-15% of daily recommended intake
- Magnesium: 15-20% of daily recommended intake

## Cooking Tips:

- Use full-fat coconut milk for a rich and creamy pudding texture. Light coconut milk may result in a thinner consistency.
- Customize the sweetness of the pudding by adjusting the amount of honey or maple syrup according to your taste preferences.
- Experiment with different flavor variations by adding spices such as cinnamon or cardamom, or flavor extracts such as almond or coconut.
- Make a large batch of coconut chia seed pudding and store it in individual containers in the refrigerator for quick and convenient breakfasts or snacks throughout the week.

## Health Benefits:

- Rich in Omega-3 Fatty Acids: Chia seeds are an excellent source of plant-based omega-3 fatty acids, which support heart health, brain function, and inflammation reduction in the body.
- High in Fiber: Chia seeds are packed with soluble fiber, which promotes digestive health, regulates blood sugar levels, and helps keep you feeling full and satisfied.
- Good Source of Calcium and Magnesium: Coconut milk provides essential minerals like calcium and magnesium, which are important for bone health, muscle function, and nerve transmission.
- Antioxidant Properties: Coconut milk contains antioxidants such as vitamin C and selenium, which help protect cells from damage caused by free radicals and oxidative stress.

# Turmeric and Ginger Oatmeal

- Time of Preparation: **10 minutes**
- Cooking Time: **10 minutes**
- Serving Units: **2 servings**

## Ingredients:

- 1 cup old-fashioned rolled oats
- 2 cups water or milk of choice (such as dairy milk, almond milk, or coconut milk)
- 1 teaspoon ground turmeric
- Half a teaspoon of powdered ginger, or one teaspoon of freshly grated ginger
- 1/2 teaspoon ground cinnamon
- An optional pinch of black pepper to improve the absorption of turmeric
- Pinch of salt
- Optional toppings: sliced banana, chopped nuts, dried fruits, honey or maple syrup, coconut flakes

## Procedures:

1. In a medium saucepan, combine the rolled oats, water or milk, ground turmeric, grated ginger, ground cinnamon, optional black pepper, and pinch of salt.
2. Over medium heat, bring the mixture to a mild boil, stirring from time to time.
3. Reduce the heat to low and simmer for 5-7 minutes, or until the oats are creamy and tender, stirring occasionally to prevent sticking.
4. Once the oats are cooked to your desired consistency, remove the saucepan from the heat.
5. Serve the turmeric and ginger oatmeal warm in bowls.

6. Garnish with your choice of toppings, such as sliced banana, chopped nuts, dried fruits, honey or maple syrup, and coconut flakes.

7. Stir the toppings into the oatmeal, if desired, and enjoy!

## Nutritional Value (per serving):

- Calories: Approximately 200-250 kcal

- Protein: 6-8 grams

- Carbohydrates: 35-40 grams

- Fiber: 5-7 grams

- Fat: 4-6 grams

- Iron: 10-15% of daily recommended intake

- Vitamin C: 2-4% of daily recommended intake

- Calcium: 10-15% of daily recommended intake

## Cooking Tips:

- To enhance the flavor and aroma of the oatmeal, toast the rolled oats in the saucepan for a few minutes before adding the liquid.

- Use freshly grated ginger for the best flavor, but ground ginger can also be used as a convenient alternative.

- For added sweetness, stir in a drizzle of honey or maple syrup to the oatmeal before serving, or use ripe mashed banana as a natural sweetener.

- Customize the oatmeal with your favorite toppings, such as chopped nuts, dried fruits, seeds, or shredded coconut, to add texture and flavor.

- Leftover oatmeal can be stored in an airtight container in the refrigerator for up to 2-3 days. Before serving, reheat gently over the stove or in the microwave.

## Health Benefits:

- Anti-Inflammatory Properties: Turmeric and ginger are both renowned for their anti-inflammatory properties, thanks to their active compound's curcumin and gingerol, which may help reduce inflammation in the body.

- Digestive Support: Ginger is known for its digestive benefits, helping to soothe the stomach, alleviate nausea, and promote healthy digestion.

- Immune Boost: Both turmeric and ginger contain antioxidants and immune-boosting properties that may help support overall immune health and protect against infections.

- Heart Health: Oats are a good source of soluble fiber, which can help lower cholesterol levels and support heart health by reducing the risk of heart disease.

- Blood Sugar Regulation: The combination of fiber, protein, and complex carbohydrates in oats helps stabilize blood sugar levels, making this oatmeal a suitable option for those with diabetes.

Indulge in this comforting and nourishing Turmeric and Ginger Oatmeal for a warming breakfast option that's packed with flavor and health benefits. With its golden hue and aromatic spices, it's sure to brighten your morning and leave you feeling energized and satisfied.

# Avocado and Egg Breakfast Bowl

- Time of Preparation: 10 minutes
- Cooking Time: 10 minutes
- Serving Units: 2 servings

## Ingredients:

- 2 ripe avocados, halved and pitted
- 4 eggs
- 1 tablespoon olive oil
- Salt and pepper to taste
- Optional toppings: diced tomatoes, sliced radishes, crumbled feta cheese, chopped cilantro, hot sauce

## Procedures:

1. In a pan over a low flame, warm the olive oil.
2. Crack the eggs into the skillet and heat until they are cooked, scrambled, or poached to your preference.
3. While the eggs are cooking, scoop out some of the flesh from each avocado half to create a larger hollow for the eggs.
4. Once the eggs are cooked, carefully transfer each egg into the hollow of an avocado half.
5. Season the avocado and egg bowls with salt and pepper to taste.
6. Garnish with your choice of toppings such as diced tomatoes, sliced radishes, crumbled feta cheese, chopped cilantro, or hot sauce.
7. Serve the avocado and egg breakfast bowls immediately, while the eggs are still warm.

## Nutritional Value (per serving):

- Calories: **Approximately 300 kcal**
- Protein: **12 grams**
- Carbohydrates: **15 grams**
- Fat: **25 grams**
- Fiber: **10 grams**

## Cooking Tips:

- Select ripe avocados that will yield slightly to gentle pressure when pressed. Avoid avocados that are too firm or too mushy.
- For a healthier option, you can bake the avocado halves in the oven for 10-15 minutes at 350°F (175°C) before adding the eggs.
- Experiment with different cooking methods for the eggs, such as frying, scrambling, or poaching, to suit your taste preferences.
- Get creative with toppings to add flavor and texture to your breakfast bowls. Try diced tomatoes, sliced radishes, crumbled feta cheese, chopped cilantro, or a drizzle of hot sauce for added zest.
- Serve the avocado and egg breakfast bowls alongside whole grain toast or a side of mixed greens for a well-rounded meal.

## Health Benefits:

- Nutrient-Rich: Avocado is packed with essential nutrients, including heart-healthy monounsaturated fats, fiber, vitamins, and minerals. Eggs are an excellent source of high-quality protein, essential amino acids, vitamins, and minerals.
- Heart Health: The monounsaturated fats in avocado and the omega-3 fatty acids in eggs contribute to heart health by helping to lower LDL (bad) cholesterol levels and reduce the risk of heart disease.
- Blood Sugar Control: The combination of healthy fats, protein, and fiber in this breakfast bowl helps stabilize blood sugar levels, providing sustained energy and preventing spikes and crashes throughout the morning.
- Weight Management: Avocado and eggs are both nutrient-dense foods that can help you stay full during weightloss journey

# Lunch Recipes

# Lentil and Vegetable Stew

- 3 cloves garlic, minced
- 2 carrots, diced
- 2 stalks celery, diced
- 1 bell pepper, diced
- 1 zucchini, diced
- 1 cup diced tomatoes (fresh or canned)
- 1 teaspoon ground cumin
- 1 teaspoon ground coriander
- 1/2 teaspoon smoked paprika
- Salt and pepper, to taste
- Finely chopped fresh parsley or cilantro for garnish (optional)

## Procedures:

1. Heat the olive oil in a big saucepan or Dutch oven over medium heat.
2. Add the diced onion and minced garlic to the pot and sauté until softened and fragrant, about 3-4 minutes.
3. Stir in the diced carrots, celery, bell pepper, and zucchini, and continue to sauté for another 5 minutes, or until the vegetables start to soften.
4. Add the diced tomatoes, ground cumin, ground coriander, smoked paprika, salt, and pepper to the pot, and stir to combine.

- Time of Preparation: 15 minutes
- Cooking Time: 40 minutes
- Serving Units: 4-6 servings

## Ingredients:

- 1 cup washed and drained dried brown lentils
- 4 cups vegetable broth or water
- 2 teaspoons coconut or olive oil
- 1 onion, diced

5. Pour in the vegetable broth or water and bring the stew to a gentle boil.

6. Once boiling, reduce the heat to low, cover, and simmer for 20-25 minutes, or until the lentils and vegetables are tender.

7. Taste and adjust seasoning as needed, adding more salt and pepper if desired.

8. Serve the lentil and vegetable stew hot, garnished with chopped parsley or cilantro if desired.

## Nutritional Value (per serving):

- Calories: Approximately 200-250 kcal
- Protein: 10-12 grams
- Carbohydrates: 30-35 grams
- Fiber: 8-10 grams
- Fat: 5-7 grams
- Vitamin A: 100-150% of daily recommended intake
- Vitamin C: 70-100% of daily recommended intake
- Iron: 15-20% of daily recommended intake

## Cooking Tips:

- To save time, you can use canned lentils instead of dried lentils. Simply rinse and drain the canned lentils before adding them to the stew during the last 10-15 minutes of cooking.

- Customize the stew with your favorite vegetables or whatever you have on hand. Other options include potatoes, sweet potatoes, spinach, kale, or mushrooms.

- For added depth of flavor, consider adding a splash of balsamic vinegar or a dollop of tomato paste to the stew.

## Health Benefits:

- High in Fiber: Lentils and vegetables are rich in dietary fiber, which supports digestive health, promotes satiety, and helps regulate blood sugar levels.

- Plant-Based Protein: Lentils are a excellent source of plant-based protein, making this stew a satisfying and nutritious option for vegetarians and vegans.

- Antioxidant-Rich: The colorful array of vegetables in this stew provides a variety of vitamins, minerals, and antioxidants that help protect against oxidative stress and inflammation in the body.

- Heart-Healthy: Lentils are low in fat and cholesterol-free, while vegetables are rich in heart-healthy nutrients like potassium and folate, making this stew a heart-healthy choice that may help lower the risk of cardiovascular disease.

- Weight Management: With its high fiber and protein content, this stew can help promote weight management by keeping you feeling full and satisfied, reducing the likelihood of overeating.

Enjoy this hearty and nourishing Lentil and Vegetable Stew as a satisfying meal option that's packed with flavor and health benefits. Whether enjoyed for lunch or dinner, it's sure to become a staple in your recipe repertoire.

# Grilled Chicken and Avocado Salad

- Time of Preparation: 20 minutes
- Cooking Time: 15 minutes
- Serving Units: 2 servings

## Ingredients:

- 2 boneless, skinless chicken breasts
- 1 tablespoon olive oil
- Salt and pepper, to taste
- 4 cups mixed salad greens (such as lettuce, spinach, arugula)
- 1 avocado, sliced
- 1 cup cherry tomatoes, halved
- 1/2 cucumber, sliced
- 1/4 red onion, thinly sliced
- 1/4 cup crumbled feta cheese (optional)
- 2 tablespoons balsamic vinegar
- 2 tablespoons extra virgin olive oil
- 1 teaspoon Dijon mustard
- 1 garlic clove, minced
- Fresh herbs (such as basil, parsley, or cilantro), chopped, for garnish (optional)

## Procedures:

1. Preheat the grill to medium-high heat.
2. Season the chicken breasts with salt and pepper after brushing them with olive oil.
3. Place the chicken breasts on the preheated grill and cook for 6-8 minutes per side, or until cooked through and no longer pink in the center. Take out of the grill and let it a few minutes to rest before slicing.

4. In a large salad bowl, combine the mixed salad greens, sliced avocado, cherry tomatoes, sliced cucumber, thinly sliced red onion, and optional crumbled feta cheese.

5. In a small bowl, whisk together the balsamic vinegar, extra virgin olive oil, Dijon mustard, minced garlic, salt, and pepper to make the dressing.

6. Pour the dressing over the salad ingredients in the bowl and toss gently to coat.

7. Divide the salad mixture between serving plates and top with sliced grilled chicken.

8. Garnish with chopped fresh herbs, if desired, and serve immediately.

## Nutritional Value (per serving):

- Calories: Approximately 350-400 kcal
- Protein: 25-30 grams
- Carbohydrates: 15-20 grams
- Fiber: 8-10 grams
- Fat: 20-25 grams
- Vitamin C: 50-70% of daily recommended intake
- Vitamin K: 100-150% of daily recommended intake
- Potassium: 20-25% of daily recommended intake

## Cooking Tips:

- Pound the chicken breasts to an even thickness before grilling to ensure they cook evenly.
- For extra flavor, marinate the chicken breasts in a mixture of olive oil, lemon juice, garlic, and herbs for 30 minutes to 1 hour before grilling.
- If you don't have access to a grill, you can cook the chicken breasts on a stovetop grill pan or in a skillet over medium-high heat for similar results.
- Customize the salad with your favorite vegetables or add-ins, such as bell peppers, olives, or grilled corn.
- To make the salad dairy-free, omit the feta cheese or replace it with a dairy-free alternative such as vegan cheese or nutritional yeast.

## Health Benefits:

- Lean Protein: Grilled chicken is a excellent source of lean protein, which is essential for muscle growth, repair, and overall health.

- Healthy Fats: Avocado provides heart-healthy monounsaturated fats, which help reduce inflammation, lower cholesterol levels, and support cardiovascular health.

- Nutrient-Dense Greens: Salad greens like lettuce, spinach, and arugula are rich in vitamins, minerals, and antioxidants, including vitamin C, vitamin K, and potassium, which support immune function, bone health, and electrolyte balance.

- Fiber-Rich Vegetables: Tomatoes, cucumbers, and red onions are all high in fiber, which promotes digestive health, regulates blood sugar levels, and helps keep you feeling full and satisfied.

- Antioxidant-Rich Dressing: The balsamic vinegar and extra virgin olive oil in the dressing provide antioxidants and healthy fats that help protect cells from damage caused by free radicals and oxidative stress.

Enjoy this Grilled Chicken and Avocado Salad as a delicious and nutritious meal option that's perfect for lunch or dinner. With its combination of protein-rich chicken, creamy avocado, crisp vegetables, and flavorful dressing, it's sure to satisfy your taste buds and nourish your body.

# Quinoa Tabbouleh with Lemon and Mint

- Time of Preparation: 15 minutes
- Cooking Time: 15 minutes
- Serving Units: 4 servings

## Ingredients:

- 1 cup quinoa, rinsed
- 2 cups water or vegetable broth
- 1 cucumber, diced
- 2 tomatoes, diced
- 1/2 red onion, finely chopped
- 1/4 cup fresh parsley, chopped
- 1/4 cup fresh mint leaves, chopped
- 1/4 cup extra virgin olive oil
- Juice of 2 lemons
- Salt and pepper, to taste

## Procedures:

1. In a medium saucepan, combine the quinoa and water or vegetable broth. Heat to a boil on a medium-high heat setting.
2. Reduce the heat to low, cover, and simmer for 12-15 minutes, or until the quinoa is tender and the liquid is absorbed.
3. Once cooked, fluff the quinoa with a fork and transfer it to a large mixing bowl to cool.
4. While the quinoa is cooling, prepare the vegetables. Dice the cucumber and tomatoes, finely chop the red onion, and chop the fresh parsley and mint leaves.
5. Add the diced cucumber, tomatoes, chopped red onion, chopped parsley, and chopped mint leaves to the bowl with the cooked quinoa.
6. In a small bowl, whisk together the extra virgin olive oil, lemon

juice, salt, and pepper to make the dressing.

7. Pour the dressing over the quinoa and vegetable mixture in the bowl, and toss gently to combine.

8. Taste and adjust seasoning as needed, adding more salt, pepper, or lemon juice if desired.

9. Serve the quinoa tabbouleh chilled or at room temperature, garnished with additional fresh herbs if desired.

## Nutritional Value (per serving):

- Calories: Approximately 250-300 kcal
- Protein: 6-8 grams
- Carbohydrates: 30-35 grams
- Fiber: 5-7 grams
- Fat: 12-15 grams
- Vitamin C: 30-40% of daily recommended intake
- Vitamin K: 50-60% of daily recommended intake
- Iron: 15-20% of daily recommended intake

## Cooking Tips:

- Be sure to rinse the quinoa thoroughly before cooking to remove any bitterness.

- You can use either white or red quinoa for this recipe, or a combination of both for added color and texture.

- To add extra flavor to the quinoa, cook it in vegetable broth instead of water.

- Customize the tabbouleh with your favorite vegetables or add-ins, such as bell peppers, olives, or chickpeas.

- For a creamier texture, you can add crumbled feta cheese or diced avocado to the tabbouleh.

## Health Benefits:

- Complete Protein: Packed with all nine necessary amino acids, quinoa is one of the few plant-based meals that can be considered a complete protein. Because of this, it's a great source of protein for vegans and vegetarians.

- High in Fiber: Quinoa is rich in dietary fiber, which promotes digestive health, regulates blood sugar levels, and helps keep you feeling full and satisfied.

- Nutrient-Dense Vegetables: Cucumber, tomatoes, red onion, parsley, and mint are all packed with vitamins, minerals, and antioxidants that support overall health and well-being.

- Heart-Healthy Fats: **Extra virgin olive oil provides heart-healthy monounsaturated fats, which help reduce inflammation, lower cholesterol levels, and support cardiovascular health.**

- Hydrating and Refreshing: **The combination of fresh lemon juice and herbs like mint adds brightness and freshness to the dish, making it a refreshing option for summer meals.**

Enjoy this flavorful and nutritious Quinoa Tabbouleh with Lemon and Mint as a light and refreshing salad option for lunch or dinner. With its vibrant colors, fresh flavors, and health-boosting ingredients, it's sure to become a favorite in your recipe rotation.

# Spicy Black Bean Soup

- Time of Preparation: 15 minutes
- Cooking Time: 30 minutes
- Serving Units: 4 servings

## Ingredients:

- 2 cans (15 ounces each) black beans, drained and rinsed
- 1 tablespoon olive oil
- 1 onion, diced
- 2 cloves garlic, minced
- 1 bell pepper, diced (any color)
- 1 jalapeño pepper, seeded and minced
- 1 teaspoon ground cumin
- 1 teaspoon chili powder
- 1/2 teaspoon smoked paprika
- Optionally added 1/4 teaspoon cayenne pepper for more spiciness.
- 4 cups vegetable broth or water
- 1 can (14.5 ounces) diced tomatoes
- Juice of 1 lime
- Salt and pepper, to taste
- Fresh cilantro, chopped, for garnish
- Greek yogurt or sour cream as a garnish (optional)
- Sliced avocado, for garnish (optional)
- Crusty bread or tortilla chips for serving

## Procedures:

1. Heat the olive oil in a big saucepan or Dutch oven over medium heat.

2. Add the diced onion to the pot and sauté for 2-3 minutes, or until softened.

3. Stir in the minced garlic, diced bell pepper, and minced jalapeño pepper, and sauté for another 2-3 minutes, until fragrant.

4. Add the ground cumin, chili powder, smoked paprika, and optional cayenne pepper to the pot, and stir to coat the vegetables in the spices.

5. Pour in the vegetable broth or water, drained and rinsed black beans, and diced tomatoes (with their juices) to the pot, and stir to combine.

6. Bring the soup to a simmer, then reduce the heat to low and let it simmer for 20-25 minutes, allowing the flavors to meld together.

7. Once the soup is cooked and the flavors have developed, use an immersion blender to blend part of the soup until smooth, leaving some whole beans and vegetables for texture.

8. Stir in the lime juice, and season the soup with salt and pepper to taste.

9. Serve the spicy black bean soup hot, garnished with chopped fresh cilantro and optional toppings such as sour cream or Greek yogurt, sliced avocado, and tortilla chips or crusty bread on the side.

## Nutritional Value (per serving):

- Calories: Approximately 250-300 kcal
- Protein: 10-12 grams
- Carbohydrates: 35-40 grams
- Fiber: 10-12 grams
- Fat: 8-10 grams
- Vitamin C: 50-70% of daily recommended intake
- Iron: 20-25% of daily recommended intake
- Potassium: 15-20% of daily recommended intake

## Cooking Tips:

- For a smoother soup texture, blend all or most of the soup until smooth using a countertop blender instead of an immersion blender. Be sure to blend in batches if using a countertop blender, and exercise caution when blending hot liquids.

- Adjust the level of spiciness by adding more or less jalapeño pepper and cayenne pepper according to your taste preferences.
- Customize the soup with additional vegetables such as corn, diced carrots, or diced sweet potatoes for added flavor and nutrition.
- Leftover soup can be stored in an airtight container in the refrigerator for up to 4-5 days, or frozen for longer storage. Before serving, reheat gently over the stove or in the microwave.

## Health Benefits:

- High in Protein and Fiber: Black beans are rich in both protein and fiber, making this soup a satisfying and nutritious option that helps promote fullness, regulate blood sugar levels, and support digestive health.
- Heart-Healthy: Black beans are low in fat and cholesterol-free, while vegetables like bell peppers and tomatoes provide heart-

healthy nutrients like vitamin C and potassium, which support cardiovascular health.

- Immune Boost: The combination of vitamin C from the vegetables and antioxidants from the spices in the soup helps support a healthy immune system and protect against illness.
- Bone Health: Black beans are a good source of iron, which is important for oxygen transport in the body, while lime juice provides vitamin C, which aids in iron absorption and helps support bone health.
- Weight Management: With its high fiber content and low-calorie density, this spicy black bean soup can help support weight management by keeping you feeling full and satisfied without excess calories.

Enjoy this flavorful and warming Spicy Black Bean Soup as a nutritious and comforting meal option that's perfect for chilly days. With its blend of protein-packed black beans, vibrant vegetables, and bold spices, it's sure to become a favorite in your soup rotation.

# Zucchini Noodles with Pesto and Cherry Tomatoes

- Time of Preparation: **15 minutes**
- Cooking Time: **10 minutes**
- Serving Units: **2 servings**

## Ingredients:

- 2 large zucchinis
- 1 cup cherry tomatoes, halved
- 1/4 cup basil pesto (store-bought or homemade)
- 2 tablespoons olive oil
- 2 cloves garlic, minced
- Salt and pepper, to taste
- Grated Parmesan cheese, for garnish (optional)
- Freshly torn basil leaves (optional garnish)

## Procedures:

1. Use a spiralizer or vegetable peeler to create zucchini noodles (zoodles) from the zucchini. If using a spiralizer, follow the manufacturer's instructions to spiralize the zucchini into noodles. If using a vegetable peeler, run the peeler along the length of the zucchini to create long, thin strips resembling noodles. Set aside.

2. In a big skillet, warm the olive oil over medium heat. Once aromatic, add the minced garlic and simmer for one to two minutes.

3. Add the zucchini noodles to the skillet and toss to coat in the garlic-infused olive oil. Cook for 3-4 minutes, stirring occasionally, until the zucchini noodles are just tender but still slightly crisp.

4. Stir in the halved cherry tomatoes and cook for another 1-2 minutes, until heated through.

5. Remove the skillet from the heat and stir in the basil pesto until the zucchini noodles and cherry tomatoes are evenly coated.

6. Season with salt and pepper to taste, adjusting the seasoning as needed.

7. Divide the zucchini noodles and cherry tomatoes between serving plates.

8. Garnish with grated Parmesan cheese and torn fresh basil leaves, if desired.

9. Serve immediately, and enjoy!

## Nutritional Value (per serving):

- Calories: Approximately 200-250 kcal
- Protein: 5-7 grams
- Carbohydrates: 10-15 grams
- Fiber: 3-5 grams
- Fat: 15-20 grams
- Vitamin C: 50-70% of daily recommended intake
- Vitamin A: 20-30% of daily recommended intake
- Calcium: 5-10% of daily recommended intake

## Cooking Tips:

- Be careful not to overcook the zucchini noodles, as they can become mushy if cooked for too long. The texture should be soft but somewhat crunchy.
- If you don't have a spiralizer or vegetable peeler, you can also use a julienne peeler or knife to create zucchini noodles by thinly slicing the zucchini lengthwise into noodle-like strips.
- Customize the dish by adding additional vegetables such as spinach, bell peppers, or mushrooms for extra flavor and nutrition.
- For a creamier sauce, stir in a tablespoon or two of heavy cream or coconut cream along with the pesto.
- To make the dish vegan, use a dairy-free pesto and omit the Parmesan cheese garnish.

## Health Benefits:

- Low in Calories: Zucchini noodles are low in calories and carbohydrates compared to traditional pasta, making them a lighter and more nutrient-dense option for those watching their calorie intake.

- **High in Fiber:** Zucchini is rich in dietary fiber, which promotes digestive health, regulates blood sugar levels, and helps keep you feeling full and satisfied.

- **Vitamins and Minerals:** Zucchini is a good source of vitamins A and C, as well as potassium, which are important for immune function, vision health, and electrolyte balance.

- **Heart-Healthy Fats:** Olive oil, a key ingredient in the pesto sauce, provides heart-healthy monounsaturated fats, which help reduce inflammation and support cardiovascular health.

- **Antioxidant-Rich:** Cherry tomatoes are packed with antioxidants such as vitamin C and lycopene, which help protect cells from damage caused by free radicals and oxidative stress.

Enjoy this light and flavorful Zucchini Noodles with Pesto and Cherry Tomatoes as a delicious and nutritious meal option that's perfect for summer. With its vibrant colors, fresh flavors, and health-boosting ingredients, it's sure to become a favorite in your recipe rotation.

# Dinner Recipes

# Baked Salmon with Asparagus

- 2 cloves garlic, minced
- 1 teaspoon lemon zest
- 1 tablespoon lemon juice
- One teaspoon of dried dill (or one tablespoon of minced fresh dill)
- Salt and pepper, to taste
- Lemon wedges, for serving
- Chopped fresh parsley or dill for garnish (optional)

- Time of Preparation: 10 minutes
- Cooking Time: 20 minutes
- Serving Units: 4 servings

## Ingredients:

- Four six-ounce salmon fillets, either skin-on or skinless
- 1 bunch asparagus, trimmed
- 2 tablespoons olive oil

## Procedures:

1. Preheat the oven to 400°F (200°C). A baking sheet can be gently oiled with olive oil or lined with parchment paper.
2. Place the salmon fillets on one half of the prepared baking sheet, leaving some space between each fillet.
3. Arrange the trimmed asparagus spears on the other half of the baking sheet, surrounding the salmon fillets.
4. In a small bowl, whisk together the olive oil, minced garlic, lemon zest, lemon juice, dried dill, salt, and pepper to make the marinade.
5. Drizzle the marinade over the salmon fillets and asparagus

spears, using your hands or a brush to evenly coat them.

6. Place the baking sheet in the preheated oven and bake for 15-20 minutes, or until the salmon is cooked through and flakes easily with a fork, and the asparagus is tender-crisp.

7. Once baked, remove the baking sheet from the oven and let the salmon and asparagus rest for a few minutes before serving.

8. Serve the baked salmon and asparagus hot, garnished with lemon wedges and chopped fresh dill or parsley, if desired.

## Nutritional Value (per serving):

- Calories: Approximately 300-350 kcal
- Protein: 30-35 grams
- Carbohydrates: 5-7 grams
- Fiber: 2-3 grams
- Fat: 18-20 grams
- Omega-3 Fatty Acids: 1-2 grams
- Vitamin D: 20-30% of daily recommended intake
- Vitamin B12: 80-100% of daily recommended intake
- Vitamin K: 70-90% of daily recommended intake

## Cooking Tips:

- Select fresh, premium salmon fillets for optimal flavor and texture. Seek for brightly colored, firm, and juicy fillets.
- If using skin-on salmon fillets, place them skin-side down on the baking sheet to prevent sticking.
- To ensure even cooking, try to select asparagus spears that are similar in thickness. If some are thicker than others, you may need to adjust the cooking time accordingly.
- Don't over-marinate the salmon and asparagus. Aim for about 10-15 minutes of marinating time to allow the flavors to penetrate without overpowering the delicate taste of the fish.
- For added flavor, you can sprinkle additional lemon zest or fresh herbs over the salmon and asparagus before serving.

## Health Benefits:

- Rich in Omega-3 Fatty Acids: Salmon is an excellent source of omega-3 fatty acids, which are essential for heart health, brain function, and reducing inflammation in the body.

- High in Protein: Salmon is packed with protein, which is important for muscle growth, repair, and overall health.

- Vitamins and Minerals: Salmon is rich in vitamins B12 and D, as well as selenium and potassium, which support immune function, bone health, and electrolyte balance.

- Antioxidant-Rich: Asparagus is loaded with antioxidants such as vitamins A, C, and E, as well as glutathione, which help protect cells from damage caused by free radicals and oxidative stress.

- Heart-Healthy: Both salmon and asparagus are low in saturated fat and cholesterol, making them heart-healthy choices that can help lower the risk of cardiovascular disease.

# Chicken and Broccoli Stir-Fry

- Time of Preparation: 15 minutes
- Cooking Time: 15 minutes
- Serving Units: 4 servings

**Ingredients:**

- 1 lb (450g) boneless, skinless chicken breast or thigh, thinly sliced
- 2 cups broccoli florets
- 1 red bell pepper, thinly sliced
- 1 small onion, thinly sliced
- 2 cloves garlic, minced
- 1 tablespoon ginger, minced
- Two tablespoons soy sauce (for a gluten-free alternative, use tamari)
- 1 tablespoon oyster sauce (optional)
- 1 tablespoon sesame oil
- 2 tablespoons vegetable oil (for stir-frying)
- Salt and pepper, to taste
- Cooked rice or noodles, for serving
- Sesame seeds and chopped green onions, for garnish (optional)

## Procedures:

1. In a small bowl, mix together the soy sauce, oyster sauce (if using), and sesame oil to create the sauce. Set aside.
2. In a large skillet or wok, heat the vegetable oil over medium-high heat.
3. Add the sliced chicken to the skillet and stir-fry for 3-4 minutes, or until it is cooked through and no longer pink. After taking the chicken out of the skillet, set it aside.

4. In the same skillet, add a little more oil if needed, then add the minced garlic and ginger. Stir-fry for 1-2 minutes, until fragrant.

5. Fill the skillet with the bell pepper, broccoli florets, and sliced onion. Stir-fry the veggies for 3–4 minutes, or until they are crisp-tender.

6. Add the cooked chicken and veggies back to the skillet.

7. Cover the chicken and veggies in the pan with the sauce. To uniformly coat everything with sauce, give it a good stir.

8. Cook for another 2-3 minutes, stirring occasionally, until everything is heated through and the sauce has thickened slightly.

9. To taste, add salt and pepper for seasoning.

10. Serve the chicken and broccoli stir-fry hot, over cooked rice or noodles.

11. Garnish with sesame seeds and chopped green onions, if desired.

## Nutritional Value (per serving without rice or noodles):

- Calories: Approximately 250-300 kcal
- Protein: 25-30 grams
- Carbohydrates: 10-15 grams
- Fiber: 3-5 grams
- Fat: 10-12 grams
- Vitamin C: 80-100% of daily recommended intake
- Vitamin K: 70-90% of daily recommended intake

## Cooking Tips:

- To make slicing the chicken easier, partially freeze it for about 20-30 minutes before cutting.
- Don't overcook the vegetables; they should be tender-crisp to retain their texture and nutrients.
- Customize the stir-fry with additional vegetables such as mushrooms, snow peas, or carrots.
- If you prefer a thicker sauce, mix 1-2 teaspoons of cornstarch with a little water and add it to the skillet along with the sauce ingredients.
- For added heat, you can add a pinch of red pepper flakes or chopped fresh chili peppers to the stir-fry.

## Health Benefits:

- **Lean Protein:** Chicken is a rich source of lean protein, which is essential for muscle growth, repair, and overall health.

- **Nutrient-Rich Vegetables:** Broccoli, red bell pepper, and onion are packed with vitamins, minerals, and antioxidants that support immune function, vision health, and cell repair.

- **Ginger and Garlic:** Both ginger and garlic have anti-inflammatory and immune-boosting properties, making them beneficial for overall health and well-being.

- **Heart-Healthy Fats:** Sesame oil contains heart-healthy monounsaturated fats and antioxidants that help reduce inflammation and support cardiovascular health.

- **Low in Calories:** This chicken and broccoli stir-fry is low in calories and carbohydrates, making it a nutritious and satisfying option for weight management and overall health.

# Stuffed Bell Peppers with Quinoa and Black Beans

- Time of Preparation: 20 minutes
- Cooking Time: 40 minutes
- Serving Units: 4 servings

## Ingredients:

- Four big bell peppers (of any color), cut in half, and seeded
- 1 cup quinoa, rinsed
- 2 cups vegetable broth or water
- Fifteen ounces (15 cans) of rinsed and drained black beans
- 1 cup corn kernels (fresh, canned, or frozen)
- 1 cup diced tomatoes (fresh or canned)
- 1 small onion, finely chopped
- 2 cloves garlic, minced
- 1 teaspoon ground cumin
- 1 teaspoon chili powder
- 1/2 teaspoon smoked paprika
- Salt and pepper, to taste
- 1/2 cup shredded cheese (such as cheddar, mozzarella, or pepper jack), optional
- Fresh cilantro or parsley, chopped, for garnish (optional)
- Greek yogurt or sour cream, for serving (optional)
- Avocado slices, for serving (optional)

## Procedures:

1. Preheat the oven to 375°F (190°C). Lightly grease a baking dish large enough to hold the halved bell peppers.
2. In a medium saucepan, combine the quinoa and vegetable broth or

water. Heat to a boil on a medium-high heat setting

3. Reduce the heat to low, cover, and simmer for 15-20 minutes, or until the quinoa is tender and the liquid is absorbed.

4. While the quinoa is cooking, prepare the filling. In a large mixing bowl, combine the black beans, corn kernels, diced tomatoes, finely chopped onion, minced garlic, ground cumin, chili powder, smoked paprika, salt, and pepper. Stir until well combined.

5. Once the quinoa is cooked, add it to the bowl with the black bean mixture and stir to combine.

6. Arrange the halved bell peppers in the prepared baking dish, cut side up.

7. Spoon the quinoa and black bean mixture evenly into each bell pepper half, pressing down gently to pack the filling.

8. If using cheese, sprinkle the shredded cheese over the stuffed bell peppers.

9. Cover the baking dish with aluminum foil and bake in the preheated oven for 25-30 minutes, or until the bell peppers are tender.

10. Remove the foil and bake for an additional 5-10 minutes, or until the cheese is melted and bubbly (if using) and the tops of the bell peppers are lightly browned.

11. Remove from the oven and let the stuffed bell peppers cool slightly before serving.

12. Garnish with chopped fresh cilantro or parsley, if desired, and serve with sour cream or Greek yogurt and avocado slices on the side.

## Nutritional Value (per serving):

- Calories: Approximately 300-350 kcal
- Protein: 12-15 grams
- Carbohydrates: 50-55 grams
- Fiber: 10-12 grams
- Fat: 6-8 grams
- Vitamin C: 150-200% of daily recommended intake
- Vitamin A: 70-90% of daily recommended intake
- Iron: 20-25% of daily recommended intake

## Cooking Tips:

- To save time, you can prepare the quinoa in advance and store it in the refrigerator until ready to use.

- Customize the filling with your favorite vegetables or add-ins, such as diced bell peppers, spinach, or diced jalapeños for extra heat.

- For a vegan version, omit the cheese or use a dairy-free cheese alternative.

- To make the stuffed bell peppers gluten-free, ensure that all ingredients, including the vegetable broth and spices, are certified gluten-free.

- Leftover stuffed bell peppers can be stored in an airtight container in the refrigerator for up to 3-4 days. Reheat gently in the microwave or oven before serving.

## Health Benefits:

- Plant-Based Protein: Black beans and quinoa are both excellent sources of plant-based protein, which is important for muscle growth, repair, and overall health.

- High in Fiber: Black beans and quinoa are rich in dietary fiber, which promotes digestive health, regulates blood sugar levels, and helps keep you feeling full and satisfied.

- Nutrient-Dense Vegetables: Bell peppers, onions, tomatoes, and corn are all packed with vitamins, minerals, and antioxidants that support immune function, vision health, and cell repair.

- Heart-Healthy: A diet rich in vegetables, whole grains, and legumes like black beans and quinoa is associated with a reduced risk of heart disease and stroke.

- Low in Saturated Fat: This dish is low in saturated fat and cholesterol, making it a heart-healthy option that's suitable for those watching their cholesterol intake.

# Cauliflower Rice with Turmeric and Peas

- Time of Preparation: 10 minutes
- Cooking Time: 15 minutes
- Serving Units: 4 servings

## Ingredients:

- 1 head cauliflower, florets separated
- 1 tablespoon olive oil or coconut oil
- 1 small onion, finely chopped
- 2 cloves garlic, minced
- 1 teaspoon ground turmeric
- 1 cup frozen peas
- Salt and pepper, to taste
- Fresh cilantro or parsley, chopped, for garnish (optional)
- Lemon wedges, for serving (optional)

## Procedures:

1. Place the cauliflower florets in a food processor and pulse until they resemble rice grains, working in batches if necessary. Alternatively, you can grate the cauliflower using a box grater.
2. Heat the olive oil or coconut oil in a large skillet over medium heat.
3. Add the finely chopped onion to the skillet and sauté for 2-3 minutes, until softened.
4. Stir in the minced garlic and ground turmeric, and cook for another 1-2 minutes, until fragrant.
5. Add the cauliflower rice to the skillet and toss to coat in the onion and turmeric mixture.

6. Cook for 5-7 minutes, stirring occasionally, until the cauliflower rice is tender but still slightly crisp.

7. Stir in the frozen peas and cook for another 2-3 minutes, until heated through.

8. Season the cauliflower rice with salt and pepper to taste, adjusting the seasoning as needed.

9. Garnish with chopped fresh cilantro or parsley, if desired, and serve with lemon wedges on the side for squeezing over the rice.

## Nutritional Value (per serving):

- Calories: Approximately 50-70 kcal
- Protein: 2-3 grams
- Carbohydrates: 5-7 grams
- Fiber: 2-3 grams
- Fat: 3-5 grams
- Vitamin C: 60-80% of daily recommended intake
- Vitamin K: 20-30% of daily recommended intake

## Cooking Tips:

- Be careful not to overprocess the cauliflower in the food processor,

as it can quickly turn into mush. Aim for a rice-like texture with some texture remaining.

- Customize the cauliflower rice with additional vegetables such as diced bell peppers, carrots, or zucchini for added flavor and nutrition.

- For a complete meal, you can add protein such as cooked chicken, shrimp, or tofu to the cauliflower rice.

- To save time, you can use pre-riced cauliflower available in many grocery stores.

- If using fresh peas instead of frozen, blanch them in boiling water for 1-2 minutes before adding them to the cauliflower rice.

## Health Benefits:

- Low in Calories and Carbohydrates: Cauliflower rice is significantly lower in calories and carbohydrates compared to traditional rice, making it a great option for those watching their calorie and carb intake.

- Rich in Fiber: Cauliflower is high in dietary fiber, which promotes digestive health, regulates blood sugar levels, and helps keep you feeling full and satisfied.

- Anti-Inflammatory Properties: Turmeric, the main spice in this dish, contains curcumin, a powerful antioxidant with anti-inflammatory properties that may help reduce inflammation in the body.

- Immune-Boosting: Peas are rich in vitamins A, C, and K, as well as antioxidants, which help support immune function and protect against illness.

- Heart-Healthy Fats: Olive oil or coconut oil provides heart-healthy monounsaturated fats, which help reduce inflammation and support cardiovascular health.

# Lentil and Sweet Potato Curry

- Time of Preparation: 15 minutes
- Cooking Time: 30 minutes
- Serving Units: 4 servings

## Ingredients:

- One cup of washed dry green or brown lentils
- 2 medium sweet potatoes, peeled and diced
- 1 onion, finely chopped
- 2 cloves garlic, minced
- 1 tablespoon ginger, minced
- 1 tablespoon curry powder
- 1 teaspoon ground turmeric
- 1 teaspoon ground cumin
- 1 can (14 ounces) coconut milk
- 1 can (14.5 ounces) diced tomatoes
- 2 cups vegetable broth or water
- 2 cups fresh spinach leaves, chopped
- Salt and pepper, to taste
- Fresh cilantro, chopped, for garnish (optional)
- Naan bread or cooked rice, to be served

## Procedures:

1. In a large pot or Dutch oven, heat a little oil over medium heat. When the onion is tender, add it and simmer it for two to three minutes.
2. Stir in the minced garlic and ginger, and cook for another minute until fragrant.
3. Add the curry powder, ground turmeric, and ground cumin to the pot, and cook for 1-2 minutes,

stirring constantly, until the spices are fragrant.

4. Pour in the coconut milk, diced tomatoes (with their juices), vegetable broth or water, rinsed lentils, and diced sweet potatoes.

5. Stir well to combine, and bring the mixture to a simmer.

6. Reduce the heat to low, cover, and let the curry simmer gently for about 20-25 minutes, or until the lentils and sweet potatoes are tender and cooked through.

7. Once the lentils and sweet potatoes are cooked, stir in the chopped fresh spinach leaves and cook for another 2-3 minutes until the spinach is wilted.

8. Season the lentil and sweet potato curry with salt and pepper to taste, adjusting the seasoning as needed.

9. Serve the curry hot, garnished with chopped fresh cilantro, and accompanied by cooked rice or naan bread.

## Nutritional Value (per serving without rice or naan):

- Calories: Approximately 300-350 kcal
- Protein: 10-15 grams
- Carbohydrates: 30-40 grams
- Fiber: 8-10 grams
- Fat: 15-20 grams
- Vitamin A: 250-300% of daily recommended intake
- Vitamin C: 30-40% of daily recommended intake
- Iron: 20-25% of daily recommended intake

## Cooking Tips:

- Be sure to rinse the lentils thoroughly before adding them to the curry to remove any debris or impurities.
- Adjust the spiciness of the curry by adding more or less curry powder according to your taste preferences.
- For a creamier curry, you can use full-fat coconut milk instead of light coconut milk.
- Customize the curry with additional vegetables such as bell peppers, carrots, or cauliflower for added flavor and nutrition.
- If you have any leftover curry, you can freeze it for longer storage or keep it in the refrigerator for up to 3–4 days in

an airtight container. Before serving, reheat gently over the stove or in the microwave.

## Health Benefits:

- Rich in Fiber: Lentils and sweet potatoes are both excellent sources of dietary fiber, which promotes digestive health, regulates blood sugar levels, and helps keep you feeling full and satisfied.

- Vitamins and Minerals: Sweet potatoes are packed with vitamins A and C, while lentils provide iron and folate, making this curry a nutrient-rich meal that supports overall health and well-being.

- Anti-Inflammatory Properties: The combination of spices such as turmeric and ginger in this curry has anti-inflammatory properties that may help reduce inflammation in the body and support joint health.

- Heart-Healthy Fats: Coconut milk provides heart-healthy medium-chain triglycerides (MCTs), which may help improve cholesterol levels and support heart health.

- Plant-Based Protein: Lentils are a good source of plant-based protein, making this curry a satisfying and nutritious option for vegetarians and vegans.

# Snacks And Small Bites

# Roasted Chickpeas with Paprika

- Time of Preparation: 10 minutes
- Cooking Time: 40 minutes
- Serving Units: 4 servings

## Ingredients:

- 2 cans (15 ounces each) chickpeas (garbanzo beans), drained, rinsed, and patted dry
- 2 tablespoons olive oil
- 1 teaspoon smoked paprika
- 1/2 teaspoon garlic powder
- 1/2 teaspoon onion powder
- 1/2 teaspoon ground cumin
- If desired, add 1/4 teaspoon cayenne pepper for more spiciness
- Salt, to taste

## Procedures:

1. Preheat the oven to 400°F (200°C). For easier cleanup, line a large baking sheet with aluminum foil or parchment paper.
2. In a large mixing bowl, combine the drained and dried chickpeas with olive oil, smoked paprika, garlic powder, onion powder, ground cumin, cayenne pepper (if using), and salt to taste. Toss until the seasonings are uniformly distributed among the chickpeas.
3. Arrange the seasoned chickpeas on the baking sheet that has been prepared in a single layer.
4. Roast the chickpeas in the preheated oven for 30-40 minutes, stirring halfway through, or until they are golden brown and crispy.

5. Remove the baking sheet from the oven and let the roasted chickpeas cool slightly before serving.

6. Serve the roasted chickpeas with paprika as a crunchy and flavorful snack or appetizer.

## Nutritional Value (per serving):

- Calories: Approximately 150-200 kcal
- Protein: 6-8 grams
- Carbohydrates: 20-25 grams
- Fiber: 5-7 grams
- Fat: 5-7 grams
- Vitamin A: 10-15% of daily recommended intake
- Vitamin C: 2-4% of daily recommended intake
- Iron: 10-15% of daily recommended intake

## Cooking Tips:

- Make sure to thoroughly dry the chickpeas with paper towels after rinsing to ensure they roast evenly and become crispy.
- Customize the seasoning to your taste preferences by adjusting the amount of smoked paprika, garlic powder, and other spices.

- For extra crispiness, you can bake the chickpeas for a few extra minutes, but be careful not to burn them.

- Store any leftover roasted chickpeas in an airtight container at room temperature for up to 3-4 days. Reheat briefly in the oven to restore crispiness before serving.

## Health Benefits:

- Rich in Protein: Chickpeas are a good source of plant-based protein, which is essential for muscle growth, repair, and overall health.

- High in Fiber: Chickpeas are also high in dietary fiber, which promotes digestive health, regulates blood sugar levels, and helps keep you feeling full and satisfied.

- Vitamins and Minerals: Chickpeas contain important nutrients such as iron, magnesium, and potassium, which support immune function, bone health, and electrolyte balance.

- Heart-Healthy: Chickpeas are low in saturated fat and cholesterol, making them a heart-healthy snack option that may help lower the risk of heart disease.

- Antioxidant-Rich: Paprika, a key ingredient in this recipe, contains antioxidants such as vitamin A and carotenoids, which help protect cells from damage caused by free radicals and oxidative stress.

Enjoy these crunchy and flavorful Roasted Chickpeas with Paprika as a satisfying and nutritious snack that's perfect for munching on-the-go or serving at parties. With their simple yet delicious seasoning and health-boosting ingredients, they're sure to become a staple in your snack repertoire.

# Coconut and Matcha Energy Balls

- Time of Preparation: 15 minutes
- Cooking Time: 0 minutes
- Chilling Time: 30 minutes
- Serving Units: Makes about 12-15 energy balls

## Ingredients:

- 1 cup rolled oats
- 1/2 cup shredded coconut (unsweetened)
- 1/4 cup almond butter (or any nut or seed butter of your choice)
- 1/4 cup honey or maple syrup
- 2 tablespoons coconut oil, melted
- 1 tablespoon matcha powder
- 1 teaspoon vanilla extract
- Pinch of salt

## Procedures:

1. In a food processor, combine the rolled oats, shredded coconut, almond butter, honey or maple syrup, melted coconut oil, matcha powder, vanilla extract, and a pinch of salt.
2. Pulse the mixture until it comes together and forms a sticky dough.
3. If the mixture seems too dry, you can add a little more almond butter or coconut oil. If it's too wet, add more rolled oats or shredded coconut.
4. Once the mixture has reached the desired consistency, use a spoon or your hands to scoop out small portions and roll them into balls.
5. To firm up, place the energy balls on a baking sheet covered with parchment paper and refrigerate for at least half an hour.

6. The energy balls are ready to eat once they have cooled. Any leftovers can be kept in the fridge for up to a week if they are kept in an airtight container.

## Nutritional Value (per serving, based on 1 energy ball):

- Calories: Approximately 100-120 kcal
- Protein: 2-3 grams
- Carbohydrates: 10-12 grams
- Fiber: 2-3 grams
- Fat: 6-8 grams
- Vitamin A: 20-30% of daily recommended intake
- Iron: 6-8% of daily recommended intake

## Cooking Tips:

- Use unsweetened shredded coconut to control the sugar content of the energy balls.
- Feel free to customize the recipe by adding other mix-ins such as chopped nuts, dried fruit, or chocolate chips.
- If you prefer a stronger matcha flavor, you can add more matcha powder to taste.

- Make sure to firmly press the mixture together when rolling the energy balls to ensure they hold their shape.
- For a smoother texture, you can process the mixture for longer in the food processor until it becomes more uniform.

## Health Benefits:

- Sustained Energy: These energy balls are packed with complex carbohydrates from the rolled oats and healthy fats from the almond butter and coconut oil, providing a steady source of energy to keep you fueled throughout the day.
- Antioxidant-Rich: Matcha powder is loaded with antioxidants called catechins, which help protect cells from damage caused by free radicals and oxidative stress.
- Digestive Health: Rolled oats are high in soluble fiber, which promotes digestive health, regulates blood sugar levels, and helps keep you feeling full and satisfied.

- **Healthy Fats:** Almond butter and coconut oil provide heart-healthy monounsaturated fats and medium-chain triglycerides (MCTs), which may help improve cholesterol levels and support heart health.

- **Vitamins and Minerals:** Matcha powder contains vitamins A, C, and E, as well as iron, calcium, and potassium, providing essential nutrients to support overall health and well-being.

# Carrot and Hummus Wraps

- Time of Preparation: **15 minutes**
- Cooking Time: **0 minutes**
- Serving Units: **2 wraps**

## Ingredients:

- 2 large whole wheat or spinach tortillas
- 1/2 cup hummus (store-bought or homemade)
- 2 medium carrots, peeled and grated
- 1/2 cucumber, thinly sliced
- 1/4 red onion, thinly sliced
- 1/2 avocado, sliced
- Handful of fresh spinach leaves
- Salt and pepper, to taste
- Optional additions: sliced bell peppers, alfalfa sprouts, shredded lettuce, or any other desired vegetables

## Procedures:

1. Lay out the tortillas on a clean work surface.
2. Spread a generous layer of hummus evenly over each tortilla, leaving a small border around the edges.
3. Arrange the grated carrots, sliced cucumber, red onion, avocado slices, and spinach leaves evenly over the hummus layer on each tortilla.
4. Season the vegetable filling with salt and pepper to taste.
5. Starting from one edge, tightly roll up each tortilla to enclose the filling and form a wrap.

6. Use a sharp knife to slice each wrap in half diagonally, if desired, to make them easier to handle.

7. Serve the carrot and hummus wraps immediately, or wrap them tightly in plastic wrap or parchment paper for later enjoyment.

## Nutritional Value (per serving, based on 1 wrap):

- Calories: Approximately 250-300 kcal
- Protein: 8-10 grams
- Carbohydrates: 30-35 grams
- Fiber: 8-10 grams
- Fat: 10-12 grams
- Vitamin A: 150-200% of daily recommended intake
- Vitamin C: 30-40% of daily recommended intake
- Iron: 10-15% of daily recommended intake

## Cooking Tips:

- Choose whole wheat or spinach tortillas for added fiber and nutrients.
- Customize the wraps with your favorite hummus flavor, such as classic, roasted red pepper, or spicy chipotle.
- Feel free to add other vegetables or toppings to the wraps according to your taste preferences.
- To prevent the wraps from becoming soggy, you can layer the spinach leaves on top of the hummus before adding the other vegetables.
- For added flavor, you can sprinkle some crumbled feta cheese or drizzle a little balsamic glaze over the vegetable filling before rolling up the wraps.

**Health Benefits:**

- Nutrient-Rich Vegetables: Carrots, cucumbers, red onions, avocado, and spinach are all packed with vitamins, minerals, and antioxidants that support overall health and well-being.
- Heart-Healthy Fats: Avocado provides heart-healthy monounsaturated fats, which help reduce inflammation and support cardiovascular health.
- Plant-Based Protein: Hummus is made from chickpeas, which are a

good source of plant-based protein, essential for muscle growth, repair, and overall health.

- Fiber-Rich: Whole wheat tortillas and vegetables are high in dietary fiber, which promotes digestive health, regulates blood sugar levels, and helps keep you feeling full and satisfied.

- Low in Calories: These wraps are relatively low in calories compared to traditional sandwich options, making them a nutritious and satisfying meal or snack option for weight management.

# Mixed Nuts and Seeds Trail Mix

- Time of Preparation: 5 minutes
- Cooking Time: 0 minutes
- Serving Units: 8 servings

## Ingredients:

- 1 cup raw almonds
- 1 cup raw cashews
- 1/2 cup pumpkin seeds (pepitas)
- 1/2 cup sunflower seeds
- 1/4 cup dried cranberries
- 1/4 cup raisins or golden raisins
- 1/4 cup chunks or pieces of dark chocolate
- Optional additions: dried apricots, dried cherries, dried blueberries, coconut flakes, or any other desired nuts or seeds

## Procedures:

1. In a large mixing bowl, combine the raw almonds, cashews, pumpkin seeds, sunflower seeds, dried cranberries, raisins, and dark chocolate chips.
2. Toss the mixture until all the ingredients are evenly distributed.
3. Transfer the mixed nuts and seeds trail mix to an airtight container or individual snack bags for easy portioning.
4. Enjoy the trail mix as a convenient and nutritious snack option for hiking, road trips, or anytime you need a quick energy boost.

## Nutritional Value (per serving, based on 1/4 cup serving size):

- Calories: Approximately 150-200 kcal
- Protein: 5-8 grams
- Carbohydrates: 10-15 grams
- Fiber: 2-4 grams
- Fat: 10-12 grams
- Vitamin E: 10-15% of daily recommended intake
- Magnesium: 10-15% of daily recommended intake
- Iron: 6-8% of daily recommended intake

## Cooking Tips:

- Use raw and unsalted nuts and seeds to control the sodium content of the trail mix.
- Customize the trail mix with your favorite nuts, seeds, and dried fruits according to your taste preferences.
- Be mindful of portion sizes, as nuts and seeds are calorie-dense foods. Stick to a serving size of about 1/4 cup to keep calorie intake in check.
- Store the trail mix in an airtight container in a cool, dry place to maintain freshness. For a longer shelf life, it may also be kept in the freezer or refrigerator.

## Health Benefits:

1. Heart-Healthy Fats: Nuts and seeds are rich in monounsaturated and polyunsaturated fats, which are heart-healthy fats that help lower LDL (bad) cholesterol levels and reduce the risk of heart disease.
2. Protein-Packed: Nuts and seeds are excellent sources of plant-based protein, essential for muscle growth, repair, and overall health.
3. Fiber-Rich: Nuts, seeds, and dried fruits are high in dietary fiber, which promotes digestive health, regulates blood sugar levels, and helps keep you feeling full and satisfied.
4. Antioxidant-Rich: Dried fruits such as cranberries and raisins, as well as dark chocolate, are loaded with antioxidants that help protect cells from damage caused by free radicals and oxidative stress.

5. Vitamins and Minerals: **Nuts and seeds are also rich in essential vitamins and minerals such as vitamin E, magnesium, and iron, which support immune function, bone health, and energy production.**

Enjoy this Mixed Nuts and Seeds Trail Mix as a convenient and nutritious snack option that's perfect for fueling your outdoor adventures or providing a quick energy boost during busy days.

# Apple Slices with Almond Butter and Cinnamon

- Time of Preparation: **5 minutes**
- Cooking Time: **0 minutes**
- Serving Units: **2 servings**

## Ingredients:

- 1 large apple (such as Granny Smith or Honeycrisp), cored and sliced
- 2 tablespoons almond butter (or any nut or seed butter of your choice)
- 1/2 teaspoon ground cinnamon
- Optional toppings: honey, maple syrup, chopped nuts, or granola

## Procedures:

1. Core the apple and slice it into thin rounds or wedges.
2. Spread a thin layer of almond butter onto each apple slice.
3. Sprinkle ground cinnamon over the almond butter-topped apple slices.
4. If desired, drizzle honey or maple syrup over the apple slices for added sweetness.
5. Optional: Sprinkle chopped nuts or granola on top for extra crunch and texture.
6. Serve the apple slices with almond butter and cinnamon immediately as a delicious and nutritious snack.

## Nutritional Value (per serving):

- Calories: **Approximately 150-200 kcal**
- Protein: **3-5 grams**

- Carbohydrates: 20-25 grams
- Fiber: 5-7 grams
- Fat: 8-10 grams
- Vitamin C: 10-15% of daily recommended intake
- **Calcium:** 4-6% of daily recommended intake
- Iron: 4-6% of daily recommended intake

## Cooking Tips:

- Choose a firm and crisp apple variety for best results, as they hold up well to slicing and dipping.
- Feel free to use any nut or seed butter you prefer, such as peanut butter, cashew butter, or sunflower seed butter.
- For added flavor, you can sprinkle a little sea salt over the almond butter before adding the cinnamon.
- Customize the toppings to your taste preferences by adding chopped nuts, granola, or dried fruit for extra texture and flavor.
- To prevent the apple slices from browning, you can squeeze a little lemon juice over them before

adding the almond butter and cinnamon.

## Health Benefits:

- Nutrient-Rich Fruit: Apples are packed with vitamins, minerals, and antioxidants, including vitamin C, potassium, and flavonoids, which help support overall health and well-being.
- Healthy Fats: Almond butter provides heart-healthy monounsaturated fats and protein, essential for muscle growth, repair, and overall health.
- Blood Sugar Regulation: Cinnamon may help regulate blood sugar levels by improving insulin sensitivity and reducing insulin resistance, making it a beneficial spice for managing diabetes and metabolic syndrome.
- Dietary Fiber: Both apples and almond butter are high in dietary fiber, which promotes digestive health, regulates bowel movements, and helps keep you feeling full and satisfied.

# 5

# Smoothies And Drinks

# Green Detox Smoothie

- 1 cup pineapple chunks (fresh or frozen)
- 1/2 cucumber, chopped
- 1 tablespoon fresh lemon juice
- 1 tablespoon chia seeds
- 1 cup coconut water or water
- Optional additions: a handful of fresh cilantro or parsley, a knob of fresh ginger, a scoop of protein powder, or a teaspoon of spirulina powder

## Procedures:

1. In a blender, combine the fresh spinach leaves, sliced banana, avocado, pineapple chunks, chopped cucumber, fresh lemon juice, chia seeds, and coconut water or water.
2. Blend on high speed until smooth and creamy, adding more liquid as needed to reach your desired consistency.
3. Taste the smoothie and adjust the flavor as desired, adding more lemon juice for acidity or a touch of honey or maple syrup for sweetness, if needed.
4. Once the smoothie is well blended and smooth, pour it into glasses and serve immediately.

- Time of Preparation: 5 minutes
- Cooking Time: 0 minutes
- Serving Units: 2 servings

## Ingredients:

- 2 cups fresh spinach leaves
- 1 ripe banana, peeled and sliced
- 1/2 avocado, pitted and peeled

## Nutritional Value (per serving):

- Calories: Approximately 150-200 kcal
- Protein: 3-5 grams
- Carbohydrates: 25-30 grams
- Fiber: 7-10 grams
- Fat: 6-8 grams
- Vitamin A: 100-150% of daily recommended intake
- Vitamin C: 80-100% of daily recommended intake
- Potassium: 15-20% of daily recommended intake
- Magnesium: 10-15% of daily recommended intake

## Cooking Tips:

- Use ripe bananas for natural sweetness and creaminess in the smoothie.
- If you prefer a colder smoothie, use frozen pineapple chunks instead of fresh, or add a handful of ice cubes to the blender.
- Customize the smoothie with additional ingredients such as fresh cilantro or parsley for added detoxifying properties, ginger for a spicy kick, protein powder for post-workout recovery, or spirulina powder for extra nutrients.
- For a thicker smoothie, use less liquid or add more avocado or banana.
- To make the smoothie ahead of time, blend all the ingredients except the liquid and chia seeds, and store the mixture in an airtight container in the refrigerator. When ready to serve, add the liquid and chia seeds, and blend until smooth.

## Health Benefits:

- Detoxifying Properties: This green smoothie is packed with detoxifying ingredients like spinach, cucumber, and lemon juice, which help cleanse the body of toxins and support liver health.
- Rich in Nutrients: Spinach, avocado, banana, and pineapple are all nutrient-dense foods that provide essential vitamins, minerals, and antioxidants, supporting overall health and well-being.
- Hydrating: Coconut water is naturally hydrating and provides electrolytes like potassium and

magnesium, making this smoothie an excellent choice for post-workout replenishment or hot summer days.

- Digestive Health: Chia seeds are high in dietary fiber, which promotes digestive health, regulates bowel movements, and helps keep you feeling full and satisfied.

- Immune Boosting: The vitamin C from the pineapple and lemon juice, along with the antioxidants from the spinach and avocado, help support immune function and protect against illness.

# Beetroot and Ginger Juice

- Time of Preparation: 10 minutes
- Cooking Time: 0 minutes
- Serving Units: 2 servings

## Ingredients:

- 2 medium-sized beetroots, peeled and chopped
- 1-inch piece of fresh ginger, peeled and chopped
- 2 medium-sized apples, cored and chopped
- 1 medium-sized carrot, peeled and chopped
- 1 tablespoon fresh lemon juice
- Optional: a pinch of ground cinnamon or a dash of cayenne pepper for added flavor

## Procedures:

1. Wash and prepare all the ingredients as instructed.
2. In a juicer, combine the chopped beetroots, ginger, apples, carrot, and fresh lemon juice.
3. Process the ingredients through the juicer until smooth and well combined.
4. Stir the juice to ensure it's well mixed.
5. If desired, add a pinch of ground cinnamon or a dash of cayenne pepper for additional flavor and heat.
6. Pour the beetroot and ginger juice into glasses and serve immediately.

## Nutritional Value (per serving):

- Calories: Approximately 100-150 kcal
- Protein: 1-2 grams
- Carbohydrates: 25-30 grams
- Fiber: 5-7 grams
- Fat: 0-1 gram
- Vitamin A: 100-150% of daily recommended intake
- Vitamin C: 50-100% of daily recommended intake
- Iron: 6-10% of daily recommended intake
- Potassium: 10-15% of daily recommended intake

## Cooking Tips:

- For optimal flavor and nutritional value, use foods that are fresh and of superior quality.
- Adjust the sweetness and tartness of the juice by adding more or fewer apples or carrots, according to your taste preferences.
- For a smoother juice texture, strain the juice through a fine-mesh sieve or cheesecloth to remove any pulp or fibrous particles.
- Serve the juice immediately after juicing to retain its freshness and maximize its nutritional benefits.

## Health Benefits:

- Heart Health: Beetroots are rich in nitrates, which help dilate blood vessels, improve blood flow, and lower blood pressure, reducing the risk of heart disease.
- Anti-Inflammatory: Ginger contains bioactive compounds with potent anti-inflammatory properties that may help reduce inflammation and alleviate symptoms of arthritis and other inflammatory conditions.
- Digestive Aid: Ginger stimulates digestion and helps relieve gastrointestinal discomfort, such as nausea, indigestion, and bloating.
- Detoxification: Beetroots support liver function and promote detoxification, helping flush toxins from the body and support overall liver health.

# Golden Milk Turmeric Latte

- 1/2 teaspoon ground cinnamon
- 1/4 teaspoon ground ginger
- 1/4 teaspoon ground cardamom
- Pinch of black pepper (enhances turmeric absorption)
- One tablespoon of maple syrup or honey, according to taste
- One teaspoon ghee or coconut oil (optional; adds extra richness)
- Optional: a dash of vanilla extract or a sprinkle of nutmeg for extra flavor

## Procedures:

1. In a small saucepan, heat the almond milk over medium heat until warmed but not boiling.
2. Add the ground turmeric, cinnamon, ginger, cardamom, black pepper, honey or maple syrup, and coconut oil or ghee to the warm milk.
3. Whisk the mixture continuously until all the ingredients are well combined and the spices are dissolved.
4. Continue to heat the turmeric latte for another 2-3 minutes, stirring occasionally, until it is steaming hot.

- Time of Preparation: 5 minutes
- Cooking Time: 5 minutes
- Serving Units: 2 servings

## Ingredients:

- Two cups of unsweetened almond milk (or any other type of milk you want)
- 1 teaspoon ground turmeric

5. Remove the saucepan from the heat and pour the golden milk turmeric latte into mugs.

6. Optional: Garnish each latte with a sprinkle of ground cinnamon, nutmeg, or a cinnamon stick for presentation.

7. Serve the golden milk turmeric latte immediately and enjoy its soothing warmth.

## Nutritional Value (per serving):

- Calories: Approximately 100-150 kcal
- Protein: 1-2 grams
- Carbohydrates: 15-20 grams
- Fiber: 1-2 grams
- Fat: 3-5 grams
- Vitamin D: 20-30% of daily recommended intake (if fortified)
- Calcium: 20-30% of daily recommended intake (if fortified)
- Iron: 4-6% of daily recommended intake

## Cooking Tips:

- Use high-quality ground spices for the best flavor and health benefits.

- Adjust the sweetness of the latte by adding more or less honey or maple syrup to suit your taste preferences.

- For added creaminess and richness, include coconut oil or ghee in the latte. However, this is optional and can be omitted for a lighter version.

- Be careful not to boil the turmeric latte, as high heat can degrade some of the beneficial compounds in the spices.

- To make a frothy latte, use a frothier or immersion blender to whip the latte until foamy before serving.

## Health Benefits:

- Anti-Inflammatory: Turmeric contains curcumin, a compound with powerful anti-inflammatory and antioxidant properties that help reduce inflammation and oxidative stress in the body.

- Digestive Aid: Ginger and cardamom are both known for their digestive benefits, helping soothe the stomach, relieve nausea, and improve digestion.

- Immune Boost: Turmeric, cinnamon, and ginger are rich in antioxidants and have immune-boosting properties that help support the body's natural defenses against infections and illnesses.

- Mood Enhancement: The warm and comforting flavors of the golden milk turmeric latte can help promote relaxation, reduce stress, and improve mood.

- Bone Health: Almond milk is often fortified with calcium and vitamin D, which are essential nutrients for bone health and strength.

# Berry Antioxidant Smoothie

- Time of Preparation: 5 minutes
- Cooking Time: 0 minutes
- Serving Units: 2 servings

## Ingredients:

- 1 cup mixed berries (such as strawberries, blueberries, raspberries, and blackberries)
- 1 ripe banana, peeled and sliced
- 1/2 cup plain Greek yogurt or dairy-free yogurt
- One tablespoon of maple syrup or honey (optional; adds sweetness)
- Half a cup of unsweetened almond milk, or any other type of milk
- 1 tablespoon chia seeds or flaxseeds (optional, for added fiber and omega-3 fatty acids)
- Handful of spinach or kale leaves (optional, for added nutrients)

## Procedures:

1. In a blender, combine the mixed berries, sliced banana, Greek yogurt, honey or maple syrup (if using), almond milk, and chia seeds or flaxseeds (if using).
2. If adding spinach or kale leaves, add them to the blender as well.
3. Blend on high speed until smooth and creamy, adding more almond milk as needed to reach your desired consistency.
4. Taste the smoothie and adjust the sweetness by adding more honey or maple syrup, if desired.
5. Once the smoothie is well blended, pour it into glasses and serve immediately.

## Nutritional Value (per serving):

- Calories: Approximately 150-200 kcal
- Protein: 5-8 grams
- Carbohydrates: 25-30 grams
- Fiber: 5-8 grams
- Fat: 3-5 grams
- Vitamin C: 50-100% of daily recommended intake
- Vitamin K: 50-100% of daily recommended intake
- Calcium: 15-20% of daily recommended intake
- Iron: 6-10% of daily recommended intake

## Cooking Tips:

- Use a variety of fresh or frozen berries for a diverse range of flavors and nutrients.
- Choose ripe bananas for natural sweetness and creaminess in the smoothie.
- For added creaminess and protein, use Greek yogurt or dairy-free yogurt.
- Customize the smoothie with additional ingredients such as chia seeds or flaxseeds for added

fiber and omega-3 fatty acids, or leafy greens like spinach or kale for added vitamins and minerals.

- To make the smoothie thicker, add more frozen berries or banana. You may thin it down by adding extra almond milk

## Health Benefits:

- Antioxidant-Rich: Berries are packed with antioxidants such as anthocyanins, flavonoids, and vitamin C, which help protect cells from damage caused by free radicals and oxidative stress.

- Immune Boost: The vitamin C from the berries and the probiotics from the Greek yogurt help support immune function and protect against infections and illnesses.
- Digestive Health: Greek yogurt is a good source of probiotics, which promote gut health by supporting the growth of beneficial bacteria in the digestive tract.
- Heart Health: Berries are low in calories and high in fiber, which helps lower cholesterol levels,

regulate blood sugar levels, and reduce the risk of heart disease.

- Bone Health: Greek yogurt is rich in calcium and vitamin D, essential nutrients for bone health and strength.

You can enjoy this refreshing and nutritious Berry Antioxidant Smoothie as a delicious and healthy way to start your day or refuel after a workout. With its vibrant colors, sweet and tangy flavors, and array of health benefits, it's sure to become a staple in your smoothie rotation.

# Lavender and Chamomile Tea

- 2 teaspoons dried chamomile flowers
- Optional: honey, lemon slices, or fresh mint leaves for added flavor

## Procedures:

1. In a small saucepan, bring the water to a gentle boil over medium heat.
2. Once the water reaches a boil, remove the saucepan from the heat.
3. Add the dried lavender flowers and chamomile flowers to the hot water.
4. Cover the saucepan with a lid and let the herbs steep for 5-10 minutes, allowing the flavors to infuse into the water.
5. After steeping, strain the tea through a fine-mesh sieve or tea strainer to remove the lavender and chamomile flowers.
6. Pour the lavender and chamomile tea into cups or mugs.
7. If desired, sweeten the tea with honey and garnish with lemon slices or fresh mint leaves for added flavor and aroma.

- Time of Preparation: 5 minutes
- Cooking Time: 5-10 minutes
- Serving Units: 2 servings

## Ingredients:

- 2 cups water
- 2 teaspoons dried lavender flowers

8. Serve the lavender and chamomile tea immediately and enjoy its soothing warmth.

## Nutritional Value (per serving):

- Calories: Approximately 0 kcal
- Protein: 0 grams
- Carbohydrates: 0 grams
- Fat: 0 grams
- Fiber: 0 grams

## Cooking Tips:

- Use high-quality dried lavender flowers and chamomile flowers for the best flavor and aroma.
- Adjust the strength of the tea by steeping the herbs for a shorter or longer period of time, according to your taste preferences.
- If you prefer a stronger flavor, you can increase the amount of dried lavender and chamomile used or steep the tea for a longer time.
- Be cautious not to over-steep the tea, as it may become bitter or overly floral in taste.
- Customize the tea with additional ingredients such as honey, lemon slices, or fresh mint leaves to suit your taste preferences.

## Health Benefits:

- Calming and Relaxing: Lavender and chamomile are both renowned for their calming and soothing properties, helping reduce stress, anxiety, and promote relaxation and sleep.
- Digestive Aid: Chamomile tea is often used to aid digestion, relieve gastrointestinal discomfort, and alleviate symptoms of indigestion, bloating, and nausea.
- Anti-Inflammatory: Both lavender and chamomile contain anti-inflammatory compounds that help reduce inflammation and soothe sore muscles and joints.
- Antioxidant-Rich: Lavender and chamomile are rich in antioxidants, which help protect cells from damage caused by free radicals and oxidative stress, supporting overall health and well-being.

# Dessert Recipes

# Dark Chocolate Avocado Mousse

- Time of Preparation: 15 minutes
- Cooking Time: 0 minutes
- Chilling Time: 1-2 hours
- Serving Units: 4 servings

## Ingredients:

- 2 ripe avocados, peeled and pitted
- 1/3 cup unsweetened cocoa powder
- A quarter of a cup of honey or maple syrup, adjusted to taste
- 1 teaspoon vanilla extract
- Pinch of salt
- 1/4 cup almond milk, unsweetened, or any other type of milk you choose
- 4 ounces dark chocolate, melted and cooled
- Optional toppings: whipped cream, fresh berries, shaved chocolate, or chopped nuts

## Procedures:

1. In a food processor or blender, combine the ripe avocados, cocoa powder, maple syrup or honey, vanilla extract, and a pinch of salt.
2. Blend the ingredients until they are smooth and creamy, stopping occasionally to scrape down the sides of the bowl to make sure everything is thoroughly mixed.
3. With the food processor or blender running, gradually add the almond milk until the mousse reaches your desired consistency. You may need to add more or less almond milk depending on the creaminess you prefer.

4. Once the mousse is smooth and creamy, add the melted dark chocolate and blend again until fully incorporated.

5. Taste the mousse and adjust the sweetness or chocolate flavor as needed by adding more maple syrup, cocoa powder, or melted chocolate.

6. Transfer the dark chocolate avocado mousse to serving bowls or glasses.

7. Cover the mousse with plastic wrap and refrigerate for at least 1-2 hours to chill and set.

8. Before serving, garnish the mousse with optional toppings such as whipped cream, fresh berries, shaved chocolate, or chopped nuts.

9. Serve the dark chocolate avocado mousse chilled and enjoy its rich and creamy texture.

## Nutritional Value (per serving):

- Calories: Approximately 200-250 kcal
- Protein: 3-5 grams
- Carbohydrates: 20-25 grams
- Fiber: 5-8 grams
- Fat: 15-20 grams
- Potassium: 10-15% of daily recommended intake
- Iron: 10-15% of daily recommended intake

## Cooking Tips:

- For the creamiest texture and finest taste, use ripe avocados. When squeezed, they ought to give slightly under mild pressure.
- Adjust the sweetness of the mousse by adding more or less maple syrup or honey according to your taste preferences.
- For a richer chocolate flavor, use high-quality dark chocolate with a cocoa content of at least 70%.
- To melt the dark chocolate, you can use a double boiler or microwave it in short bursts, stirring frequently until smooth.
- Be patient when blending the mousse to ensure a smooth and creamy texture. You may need to stop and scrape down the sides of the bowl several times.
- Chill the mousse in the refrigerator for at least 1-2 hours before serving to allow it to set and develop its flavors.

## Health Benefits:

- Heart-Healthy Fats: Avocados are rich in monounsaturated fats, which are heart-healthy fats that help lower LDL (bad) cholesterol levels and reduce the risk of heart disease.

- Antioxidant-Rich: Dark chocolate is loaded with antioxidants, such as flavonoids, which help protect cells from damage caused by free radicals and oxidative stress.

- Fiber-Packed: Both avocados and cocoa powder are high in dietary fiber, which promotes digestive health, regulates blood sugar levels, and helps keep you feeling full and satisfied.

- Potassium Source: Avocados are a good source of potassium, an essential mineral that helps regulate blood pressure, muscle function, and fluid balance in the body.

- Mood Booster: Dark chocolate contains compounds that stimulate the production of endorphins, the feel-good hormones, promoting a sense of well-being and happiness.

# Baked Apples with Cinnamon and Walnuts

- Time of Preparation: 15 minutes
- Cooking Time: 40 minutes
- Serving Units: 4 servings

## Ingredients

- 4 large apples (such as Granny Smith or Honeycrisp)
- 1/4 cup chopped walnuts
- 2 tablespoons maple syrup or honey
- 1 tablespoon unsalted butter or coconut oil, melted
- 1 teaspoon ground cinnamon
- Pinch of ground nutmeg (optional)
- Pinch of salt

## Procedures:

1. Preheat your oven to 375°F (190°C).
2. Wash the apples and pat them dry.
3. Using an apple corer or a paring knife, carefully core each apple, removing the seeds and creating a well in the center.
4. In a small bowl, mix together the chopped walnuts, maple syrup or honey, melted butter or coconut oil, ground cinnamon, nutmeg (if using), and a pinch of salt.
5. Stuff each cored apple with the walnut mixture, dividing it evenly among the apples.
6. Place the stuffed apples in a baking dish or on a baking sheet lined with parchment paper.
7. Bake the apples in the preheated oven for about 35-40 minutes, or

until they are tender and the filling is bubbly and caramelized.

8. Once baked, remove the apples from the oven and allow them to cool for a few minutes before serving.

9. Serve the baked apples warm, optionally topped with a scoop of vanilla ice cream or a dollop of whipped cream.

## Nutritional Value (per serving):

- Calories: Approximately 180-200 kcal
- Protein: 2-3 grams
- Carbohydrates: 25-30 grams
- Fiber: 5-7 grams
- Fat: 8-10 grams
- Vitamin C: 10-15% of daily recommended intake
- Vitamin A: 4-6% of daily recommended intake
- Calcium: 2-4% of daily recommended intake
- Iron: 4-6% of daily recommended intake

## Cooking Tips:

- Choose large apples that are firm and slightly tart for the best results.
- You can leave the skins on the apples for added texture and fiber, or peel them if you prefer.
- If you don't have an apple corer, you can carefully use a paring knife to core the apples.

## Health Benefits:

- Rich in Fiber: Apples are an excellent source of dietary fiber, which helps promote digestive health, regulate bowel movements, and keep you feeling full and satisfied.
- Antioxidant-Rich: Both apples and walnuts are rich in antioxidants, such as vitamin C and polyphenols, which help protect cells from damage caused by free radicals and oxidative stress.
- Heart-Healthy Fats: Walnuts are high in omega-3 fatty acids, which have been linked to improved heart health, reduced inflammation, and lower cholesterol levels.

# Chia Seed Pudding with Mango and Lime

- Time of Preparation: 10 minutes (plus chilling time)
- Cooking Time: 0 minutes
- Chilling Time: 2-4 hours
- Serving Units: 4 servings

## Ingredients:

- 1/2 cup chia seeds
- 2 cups unsweetened coconut milk or almond milk
- 2 tablespoons maple syrup or honey (adjust to taste)
- 1 teaspoon vanilla extract
- 1 ripe mango, peeled and diced
- Zest and juice of 1 lime
- Optional toppings: sliced mango, lime wedges, shredded coconut, or chopped nuts

## Procedures:

1. In a mixing bowl, combine the chia seeds, coconut milk or almond milk, maple syrup or honey, and vanilla extract.
2. Whisk the mixture together until well combined, ensuring that there are no lumps of chia seeds.
3. Let the chia seed mixture sit for a few minutes, then whisk again to prevent clumping.
4. Cover the bowl with plastic wrap or transfer the mixture to individual jars or serving glasses.
5. Refrigerate the chia seed pudding for at least 2-4 hours, or overnight, to allow it to thicken and set.
6. While the pudding is chilling, prepare the mango topping. In a separate bowl, combine the diced mango with the lime zest and

juice. Toss to coat the mango evenly.

7. Once the chia seed pudding has chilled and set, remove it from the refrigerator.

8. Serve the chia seed pudding topped with the mango-lime mixture.

9. Garnish with additional toppings such as sliced mango, lime wedges, shredded coconut, or chopped nuts, if desired.

10. Enjoy the chia seed pudding with mango and lime immediately, or store any leftovers in the refrigerator for up to 2-3 days.

## Nutritional Value (per serving):

- Calories: Approximately 200-250 kcal
- Protein: 4-6 grams
- Carbohydrates: 20-25 grams
- Fiber: 8-10 grams
- Fat: 10-12 grams
- Vitamin C: 50-100% of daily recommended intake
- Calcium: 15-20% of daily recommended intake
- Iron: 10-15% of daily recommended intake

## Cooking Tips:

- Use a 2:1 ratio of liquid to chia seeds to achieve the desired pudding consistency. Adapt the sweetener quantity to your personal taste preferences.

- Stir the chia seed mixture well before refrigerating to ensure that the seeds are evenly distributed and do not clump together.

- For a creamier pudding, use full-fat coconut milk instead of almond milk.

- Feel free to customize the pudding with additional flavorings such as cinnamon, nutmeg, or cardamom for added depth of flavor.

- When preparing the mango topping, choose ripe and juicy mangoes for the best flavor. You can also substitute mango with other fruits such as berries, pineapple, or kiwi.

- Serve the chia seed pudding with mango and lime as a healthy breakfast, snack, or dessert option.

## Health Benefits:

- Rich in Fiber: Chia seeds are packed with dietary fiber, which helps promote digestive health, regulate bowel movements, and keep you feeling full and satisfied.

- Omega-3 Fatty Acids: Chia seeds are one of the best plant-based sources of omega-3 fatty acids, which are essential for brain health, heart health, and reducing inflammation in the body.

- Antioxidant-Rich: Mangoes and lime are rich in vitamin C and other antioxidants, which help boost the immune system, protect cells from damage caused by free radicals, and support overall health.

- Bone Health: Calcium from the chia seeds and coconut milk contributes to bone health, while vitamin C from the mangoes and lime aids in collagen production and bone strength.

- Hydration: Coconut milk and mangoes are hydrating foods, providing essential electrolytes such as potassium and magnesium, which help maintain fluid balance in the body and support hydration.

Delight in the refreshing and tropical flavors of this Chia Seed Pudding with Mango and Lime, a nutritious and satisfying treat that's perfect for any time of day. With its creamy texture, vibrant colors, and array of health benefits, it's sure to become a favorite in your recipe collection.

# Almond Flour Brownies

- Time of Preparation: 15 minutes
- Cooking Time: 25-30 minutes
- Serving Units: 9 brownies

## Ingredients:

- Half a cup of melted unsalted butter or coconut oil
- 3/4 cup granulated sugar or coconut sugar
- 2 large eggs, at room temperature
- 1 teaspoon vanilla extract
- 1/2 cup unsweetened cocoa powder
- 1/2 cup almond flour
- 1/4 teaspoon baking powder
- 1/4 teaspoon salt
- Half a cup of chopped or dark chocolate chips
- Optional: chopped nuts, sea salt flakes for topping

## Procedures:

1. Preheat your oven to 350°F (175°C). An 8x8-inch baking pan should be greased or lined with parchment paper.
2. In a mixing bowl, combine the melted butter or coconut oil with the coconut sugar or granulated sugar. Stir until well combined.
3. Add the eggs and vanilla extract to the sugar mixture, and whisk until smooth and creamy.
4. In a separate bowl, sift together the cocoa powder, almond flour, baking powder, and salt.
5. The brownies will continue to cook a little bit as they cool, so take care not to overbake them. When a toothpick is pushed into

the middle, moist crumbs rather than wet batter should come out. Be careful not to overmix.

6. Fold in the dark chocolate chips or chopped chocolate until evenly distributed throughout the batter.

7. Pour the batter into the prepared baking pan, spreading it out evenly with a spatula.

8. If desired, sprinkle chopped nuts or sea salt flakes over the top of the brownie batter for added texture and flavor.

9. Bake the brownies in the preheated oven for 25-30 minutes, or until the edges are set and a toothpick inserted into the center comes out with moist crumbs.

10. Remove the brownies from the oven and allow them to cool in the pan for at least 10-15 minutes before slicing and serving.

## Nutritional Value (per brownie):

- Calories: Approximately 200-250 kcal
- Protein: 3-5 grams
- Carbohydrates: 20-25 grams
- Fiber: 2-4 grams
- Fat: 12-15 grams

- Iron: 10-15% of daily recommended intake
- Calcium: 2-4% of daily recommended intake

## Cooking Tips:

- Use high-quality cocoa powder for the best chocolate flavor in the brownies.
- If you prefer a sweeter taste, you can increase the amount of sugar or use a combination of coconut sugar and granulated sugar.
- Make sure the eggs are at room temperature before adding them to the batter to ensure even mixing and a smoother texture.
- Almond flour adds moisture and a slightly nutty flavor to the brownies. If you don't have almond flour, you can substitute it with an equal amount of all-purpose flour or gluten-free flour blend.
- The brownies will continue to cook a little bit as they cool, so take care not to overbake them. When a toothpick is pushed into the middle, moist crumbs rather than wet batter should come out.

- For a fudgier texture, slightly underbake the brownies and allow them to cool completely before slicing.
- Store any leftover brownies in an airtight container at room temperature for up to 3-4 days, or freeze them for longer storage.

## Health Benefits:

- Gluten-Free: Almond flour is naturally gluten-free, making these brownies suitable for those with gluten sensitivities or celiac disease.
- Lower Glycemic Index: Coconut sugar has a lower glycemic index compared to refined sugar, which means it causes a slower and more gradual rise in blood sugar levels.
- Rich in Antioxidants: Dark chocolate contains antioxidants such as flavonoids, which help protect cells from damage caused by free radicals and oxidative stress.
- Heart-Healthy Fats: Almond flour and coconut oil are both sources of heart-healthy fats, including monounsaturated and medium-chain triglycerides (MCTs), which may help improve cholesterol levels and reduce the risk of heart disease.
- Protein and Fiber: Almond flour is higher in protein and fiber compared to traditional wheat flour, helping to promote satiety, regulate blood sugar levels, and support digestive health.

Enjoy the rich and indulgent flavors of these Almond Flour Brownies, a healthier twist on the classic dessert that's sure to satisfy your chocolate cravings. With their fudgy texture, intense chocolate flavor, and wholesome ingredients, they're the perfect treat for any occasion.

# 14 – Days Meal Plan

### Day 1

- **Breakfast:** Green Smoothie
- **Lunch:** Grilled Chicken and Avocado Salad
- **Snack:** Roasted Chickpeas with Paprika
- **Dinner:** Baked Salmon with Asparagus

### Day 2

- **Breakfast:** Quinoa and Berry Breakfast Bowl
- **Lunch:** Lentil and Vegetable Stew
- **Snack:** Coconut and Matcha Energy Balls
- **Dinner:** Chicken and Broccoli Stir-Fry

### Day 3

- **Breakfast:** Avocado and Egg Breakfast Bowl
- **Lunch:** Quinoa Tabbouleh with Lemon and Mint
- **Snack:** Carrot and Hummus Wraps
- **Dinner:** Stuffed Bell Peppers with Quinoa and Black Beans

### Day 4

- **Breakfast:** Turmeric and Ginger Oatmeal
- **Lunch:** Spicy Black Bean Soup
- **Snack:** Mixed Nuts and Seeds Trail Mix
- **Dinner:** Cauliflower Rice with

Turmeric and Peas

### Day 5

- **Breakfast:** Coconut Chia Seed Pudding
- **Lunch:** Zucchini Noodles with Pesto and Cherry Tomatoes
- **Snack:** Apple Slices with Almond Butter and Cinnamon
- **Dinner:** Lentil and Sweet Potato Curry

### Day 6

- **Breakfast:** Green Smoothie
- **Lunch:** Grilled Chicken and Avocado Salad
- **Snack:** Roasted Chickpeas with Paprika
- **Dinner:** Baked Salmon with Asparagus

### Day 7

- **Breakfast:** Quinoa and Berry Breakfast Bowl
- **Lunch:** Lentil and Vegetable Stew
- **Snack:** Coconut and Matcha Energy Balls
- **Dinner:** Chicken and Broccoli Stir-Fry

### Day 8

- **Breakfast:** Avocado and Egg Breakfast Bowl
- **Lunch:** Quinoa Tabbouleh with Lemon and Mint
- **Snack:** Carrot and Hummus Wraps
- **Dinner:** Stuffed Bell Peppers with

| |
|---|
| Quinoa and Black Beans |

| **Day 9** |
|---|
| • **Breakfast:** Turmeric and Ginger Oatmeal |
| • **Lunch:** Spicy Black Bean Soup |
| • **Snack:** Mixed Nuts and Seeds Trail Mix |
| • **Dinner:** Cauliflower Rice with Turmeric and Peas |

| **Day 10** |
|---|
| • **Breakfast:** Coconut Chia Seed Pudding |
| • **Lunch:** Zucchini Noodles with Pesto and Cherry Tomatoes |
| • **Snack:** Apple Slices with Almond Butter and Cinnamon |
| • **Dinner:** Lentil and Sweet Potato Curry |

| **Day 11** |
|---|
| • **Breakfast:** Green Smoothie |
| • **Lunch:** Grilled Chicken and Avocado Salad |
| • **Snack:** Roasted Chickpeas with Paprika |
| • **Dinner:** Baked Salmon with Asparagus |

| **Day 12** |
|---|
| • **Breakfast:** Quinoa and Berry Breakfast Bowl |
| • **Lunch:** Lentil and Vegetable Stew |
| • **Snack:** Coconut and Matcha Energy Balls |
| • **Dinner:** Chicken and Broccoli Stir- |

| |
|---|
| Fry |

| **Day 13** |
|---|
| • **Breakfast:** Avocado and Egg Breakfast Bowl |
| • **Lunch:** Quinoa Tabbouleh with Lemon and Mint |
| • **Snack:** Carrot and Hummus Wraps |
| • **Dinner:** Stuffed Bell Peppers with Quinoa and Black Beans |

| **Day 14** |
|---|
| • **Breakfast:** Turmeric and Ginger Oatmeal |
| • **Lunch:** Spicy Black Bean Soup |
| • **Snack:** Mixed Nuts and Seeds Trail Mix |
| • **Dinner:** Cauliflower Rice with Turmeric and Peas |

**NOTE:**

*Please consult with your healthcare provider before starting this 14-day meal plan, especially if you have any existing medical conditions or dietary restrictions. Individual nutritional needs may vary, and it's important to ensure the plan aligns with your health goals. Adjust portion sizes as needed to fit your personal energy requirements.*

# Conclusion

As you reach the end of your journey through the "Cortisol Detox Diet Cookbook 2024," take a moment to reflect on the transformative experience you've undergone. Your commitment to balance and well-being has led you on a path of discovery, empowering you to take control of your health and vitality.

Throughout this cookbook, you've explored the intricate relationship between cortisol, stress, and nutrition, gaining insights into how simple dietary adjustments can profoundly impact your physical and mental well-being. By embracing whole foods, nourishing recipes, and mindful eating practices, you've learned to harness the power of nutrition to support optimal cortisol levels and promote overall vitality.

As you move forward, remember that sustaining your cortisol detox is not merely a short-term endeavor but a lifelong commitment to self-care and holistic wellness. Continue to prioritize nutrient-rich foods, stress management techniques, regular physical activity, and adequate rest to keep your cortisol levels in check and maintain a balanced, vibrant life.

To ensure long-term success on your cortisol detox journey, cultivate habits that support your body's natural rhythms and resilience. Practice mindfulness and stress reduction techniques such as meditation, yoga, or deep breathing exercises to cultivate a sense of calm and inner peace. Prioritize sleep hygiene and create a restful bedtime routine to promote quality sleep and rejuvenation. Stay connected with your body's signals, honoring its needs for nourishment, movement, rest, and relaxation.

For those eager to delve deeper into the science behind cortisol regulation, stress management, and nutritional strategies for optimal health, a wealth of resources awaits. Explore reputable books, articles, podcasts, and online resources authored by experts in the fields of nutrition, wellness, and integrative medicine. Arm yourself with knowledge and continue to expand your understanding of how to best support your body and mind on your journey to well-being.

As you bid farewell to this cookbook, express gratitude for the abundance of nourishment, inspiration, and support it has provided on your path to wellness. Embrace the lessons learned, the flavors savored, and the moments of connection shared with loved ones around the table. Carry forward the wisdom gained and the recipes cherished as you embark on the next chapter of your health journey with gratitude, resilience, and an unwavering commitment to vibrant living.

Farewell, dear reader, and may your path be filled with continued health, joy, and vitality.

With heartfelt gratitude and warm wishes,

Grace Mitchell

Made in the USA
Columbia, SC
07 September 2024

41974148R00057